D1668490

INDIES UNITED PUBISHING HOUSE
PRESENTS

Infinite Indies

A MULTI-AUTHOR ANTHOLOGY

INDIES UNITED PUBLISHING HOUSE, LLC

ISBN13: 978-1-64456-213-0
Library of Congress Control Number: 2020948204

INDIES UNITED PUBLISHING HOUSE, LLC
P.O. BOX 3071
QUINCY, IL 62305-3071
www.indiesunited.net

TABLE OF CONTENTS

Foreword

Jennie Rosenblum

Long ago a little girl dreamed of being a librarian. As time passed, the world had a different idea, and even though that dream came true for a while – her real dream came true when she discovered the world of Independent Authors. Who thinks that, at a certain age, starting anew is the way to go?

I had been on the fringe of the self-publishing world for almost ten years. I saw the evolution but did not know the entirety of the world. So my journey began. I learned as much about the publishing world as I could, and the more I looked, the more gaping holes I saw. Many undiscovered gem-type authors and their wonderful stories were not making it in the traditional publishing world and so instead, they were trying to figure out their way in self-publishing. I wanted to help but there was little out there that either didn't require a lot of money or could be depended upon.

Then I had a conversation, well several actually, with Lisa Orban. She had an idea she thought could work. I happily watched from the sidelines, throwing in my two cents as she did all the heavy lifting and her dream became reality. Her creation, Indies

United Publishing, provides a base for authors. They can be independent but at the level with which they are comfortable. Indies United provided solutions and freedoms at a reasonable cost. No more going it all alone. And best of all, it was a place I could send those special authors!

Back in my world, I was collecting Indie authors. At one point someone called me the Kevin Bacon of the Indie world and I took that compliment with a smile. Like trading cards, each author is unique; they just do not fit well into a shoebox. I have a connection with each. Some of them have been to my home for dinner, many I have shared a cup of tea with, and there may have been a gin with one or two – but I'll never tell. Some I have only met through the pages of their creations, but even that helps me know them.

First in my collection is the original Aaron Gallagher. Over very strong tea, we discussed his characters and his vision. The first book I read of his is still a favorite but this author has honed his skills to a level where I would put him up against any New York Times Bestseller. (Please do not mention that to him as it will only go to his head!) He was quickly followed by Sosha Ruark, another cup, this time iced tea, and a discussion on how her mind worked and a vision of a trilogy.

After taking care of my mother as she passed and trying to help my Dad get ready for life on his own, I discovered the *I'd Rather Starve than Cook!* Cookbook and Lisa Orban. With a unique voice and grandiose ideas, I quickly added her to my quiver.

She is fun and real and I crave people like that in my life.

An email from across the pond (thank you Claire Perkins) brought the thought provoking R.J. Emery into my circle. With a wit that keeps me amused and a mind that is spinning I have hung on his coattails and enjoyed the view.

A trip to Tucson and their Festival of books introduced me to a gentleman (again, don't let him know I said that as he likes to think of himself as a bit of an asshole) who was giving away absolutely free business cards. Ok, make me laugh and I am halfway there to liking you! His *Calizona* series sealed the deal, entertained me, and I kept an eye on this guy too.

Advance about two years, my editing business is picking up and I am finally making more than I am spending – so I went to Orlando and their Indie Book Fest. Through days and many conversations about way too much romance, I see a cover that catches my eye. The author has an idea for a Pulp fiction collection of other authors. I had a tie to Indies United (remember Lisa?) and thought it would be right up their alley. Plus, he was a really nice guy, and had some great stories – enter Scott Meehan.

Lisa introduced me to the work of Guy Thair, J. B. Murray, Timothy Baldwin, and Dr. Wood. Guy and JB over some decent barbeque and a few boozy drinks. Timothy came along a little later when his first YA book *Camp Lenape* was released. Dr. Wood stretches my thinking with every paragraph. Each author has a unique voice with a very different story to tell, and all with that something extra that lets you know it's going to be a great story.

Muhammad Idrees found me and after hearing his story and reading of his unique adventures in Kyrgyzstan, I introduced him to Indies United. There was nothing like his story in the publishing world.

Mike Deeze (or Dr. Mike as I think of him) had me hooked with his trilogy. His third has wonderful stories that took me right back to my college days in central Pennsylvania when I would go home for weekend trips with my roommates and hear the Amish buggies passing their house after date nights. Editing that book was tough as I kept dreaming about Shoo-Fly Pie!

Ketan Desai is the most recent one added to my collection, but definitely not the least or last. His book, *Germs of War*, a bioterrorism thriller, kept me firmly in my seat and swiping pages. His logical presentation of a scary scenario was right on point.

Being a person who mostly deals in organization and logic, I find the world of authors and their creativity intriguing. Any chance to glance behind the proverbial curtain and discover each creation keeps me entertained and motivated. However, my absolute favorite thing to read is an anthology. That giant box of chocolates that Forest Gump waxes poetic about is my chance to test out various authors, styles, and genres.

So grab your favorite beverage, find a comfortable spot, and crack the spine on this impressive collection of chocolates… ummm… stories.

Feel free to see all my reading suggestions at jenniereads.com or contact me if I can help in any way to make your dream of publishing come true. I'm always ready for the next Author and story!

Why Do We Write?

R.J. Emery

That's a question I think every author asks more often than not. On good days I know why I write. On the bad days, when I can't get what's in my head down on the page, not so much. Comedy is easy, writing is hard. I've been at it since 2006 and I'm still learning.

I began writing short stories at the tender age of 13. I wrote about things that interested me. Sometimes it was a couple of pages, sometimes more. The first was about the loss of my dog who had been run over by a passing truck. Yeah, I know, gruesome. The other early stories are just a foggy memory. I wish I had kept them.

I attended a Catholic school where we had great nuns for teachers. One, in particular, Sister Mary Dora, read my stories and encouraged me to keep writing. She asked me one day why I enjoyed it so much. I answered with a shrug. She said, "I know why, because you have stories to tell." (A line I actually included in Swimming Upstream, a feature film I wrote and directed). With Sister Dora's encouragement, those little stories expanded into 5, 6, 7 pages. I kept on writing all through the years including the 4 years I served in the Air Force. There, I found another mentor, the 1st Lieutenant who was my immediate supervisor. He, like Sisters Dora, read my short stories and encouraged me to keep writing.

It was during this time I took an interest in films and wrote my first screenplay. It was awful. It wasn't until I was a civilian working in advertising writing newspaper and radio copy that I penned a screenplay that actually got produced with private investor backing. Since the film was my vision, I was encouraged to direct. I was petrified—I had no idea what I was doing. Thank goodness for the professional film crew who looked after this newbie or I would have never made it through. If not for them, I'd probably be selling timeshare condos today.

Seven features films later—all of which I wrote and directed—and over 140 hours of award-winning television productions and more TV commercials than I care to remember—I retired. A New York publisher offered to publish my memories of a television series I created, wrote, and directed for Starz/Encore titled "The Directors." I wrote and directed ninety-one episodes. Each featured a single film director along with over 250 major Hollywood actors, composers, and cinematographers. I ended up writing four volumes on those experiences. Suddenly I was a published author. But there was one screenplay I wanted to see produced that did not get picked up. An author friend encouraged me to turn it into a novel instead. I had no experience writing fiction, but I wrote the book over two years and a publisher picked it up. I'm now working on my 4th and 5th novels and another non-fiction in the works. So many stories to tell, so little time.

Each of us approaches our writing in our own way. My method is to never outline my novels. I know my main characters and the opening and the ending. From there, I allow my imagination to take over surprising myself chapter after chapter. I love the freedom of working that way. I do take copious notes about points I want to make, but never an outline.

For me, the most important thing is creating believable characters; without them, the story is just another story. I plead guilty to being a "rewriter." No book is ever really finished, so I depend on my wife who reads everything I write and eventually forces me to stop and send it to my editor.

There are two themes here. First, I had people who encouraged me. That was critical. And although I had many years of experience writing screenplays and TV scripts, I had zero experience writing novels before that first one but found that I loved it. Today, I spend 4-6 hours a day writing, I reminding myself each day how fortunate I am doing what I love.

So, as Sister Dora said, we write because we have stories to tell. It's that simple. Let's keep doing it.

To find out more about R.J. Emery and his books, visit
www.indiesunited.net/rj-emery

Spring

NONFICTION

A Girl Alone

Scott Meehan

An American Army Officer reflects on his experience in Iraq with insight on those who helped.

"A trustworthy envoy brings healing."
—Proverbs 13:17

In 2003, American forces arrived in Iraq and overthrew the regime of Saddam Hussein. Many Iraqi people celebrated the American victory with renewed freedom from oppression and a number of them were brave enough to risk everything to help the Americans rebuild their country. This is a story of one such girl whose father, mother, brother, and sister arrived in America to begin a new life because their lives were in danger in their home country of Iraq. Yet, this girl, Amal, was left behind due to her age and now faces life threatening dangers on a daily basis.

Towards the end of my 25-year military career, I

wanted nothing more than to finish my tour in Iraq and return home in one piece. But when the people of the country that we invaded looked to me for some semblance of hope and a chance of having peace, I put my heart and soul into building trust through compassion and care while doing everything in my power to bring that hope and peace to their lives. Yet, the stakes were deadly for the those who were identified as ones who befriended an American soldier.

I departed the veiled Kingdom of the Arabian Peninsula and the 140-degree heat, after four months. On my way to a new destination, Iraq, I felt as if I was going from the frying pan to the fire... there was an all-out war in Iraq.

As the C-130 descended, I peered through the small portal of the aircraft and saw a land forsaken—void of springs, foliage, and living water. Saudi Arabia was no different. Both places could easily pass for the dark side of the moon.

Clothed in various brown and tan patterns identified me as a soldier. With the red, white, and blue flag sewn on my shoulder...an American soldier.

Our plane continued to descend into a corkscrew spiral. The Balad Airbase loomed below, surrounded by stretches of barren desert and patches of verdant farmland. Groves of date palms pocketed the northern areas. An Airman approached me. "Sir, we're starting our final approach if you'll take your seat please."

I nodded my head and tried not to stumble my

way back to the olive-colored canvas seats attached to the red-strapped backrest. Daylight was fading. Darkness would soon cover the earth.

The hot sun baked the desert sand, reaching temperatures of 130 degrees Fahrenheit during the summer. The wintry rainy season was cold, damp, and miserable. The dried, powdered, dusty sand turned into a muddy quagmire during the rainy season.

God tested me in one place to refine me in the other. It was during my time in Iraq, amidst the nearly daily rockets and mortars landing onto our base at Camp Anaconda, I learned the Iraqi culture...not Sunni, Shi'a, Kurdish, or Christian, but Iraqi—through the eyes of entrepreneurs...both young and old.

I was assigned as a Contingency Contracting Officer and my job was to procure the best products, supplies, and services from local businesses for our American service members, both men and women. Highlights included hundreds of contracts that supplied hard armored bullet-proof steel, which was installed on our transport vehicles. Other popular items were the portable Electric Control Units (ECUs) that kept our soldiers cool in the blazing heat and warm in the bitter cold. Our forces amounted to more than twenty-five thousand in our sector alone.

By learning the Iraqi business culture, including their language, I succeeded in building and establishing a long-term and wide range of trust. The ultimate show of trust, at the risk of their own lives, was when locals confided in me...like the time when the information being relayed led to the whereabouts and capture of their former president—Saddam Hussein himself.

That was when a vendor approached me one day and let me know that he had cousins in Baghdad who had very important information that they needed to tell me. He said that they did not trust Americans but that he convinced them that they could trust me. So, they agreed to travel to Balad from Baghdad—a dangerous trek, to share their knowledge.

When they arrived the next day, the four of us departed the crowds and went to an empty field. "What would you like to tell me?" I asked.

The vendor translated my question in Arabic to the two men. One of them explained something in Arabic.

Turning to me, the vendor spoke. "He said that they know where one of Saddam's hideouts is in Baghdad. It is a safe house with his officers and members of his team."

"This is very important information," I told him. As discussed, the day before, I reminded him, "They will still tell my friends this story?"

The vendor looked at them and asked a question in Arabic. They both agreed. He looked at me and nodded his head.

"Come on," I said in Arabic. "Follow me."

I brought them to a pre-arranged room with three members of the military intelligence community waiting...and left them there. Two hours later, they returned to my contracting office. We had a small discussion—outside the building, and then they departed. I never saw any of them again.

Ten days later—several miles to the north under a moonless night, approximately six hundred soldiers from the 4th Infantry Division (ID) began a raid in the small town of Ad Dawr. When the soldiers found a hole partially buried, they uncovered it and to their disbelief, they saw a beleaguered old man with a scraggly gray and white beard.

"I am Saddam Hussein; I am the president of Iraq! I want to negotiate," the man said in English.

Days later, I discovered that one of Hussein's drivers told the Americans where he was hiding. Where did they find this driver? Soldiers rounded him up in the Baghdad safe house along with many others…the same safe house known by the vendor's "cousins."

Five more months went by, slowly, and then, my tour of duty was over. It had been a very long year. I was going home…hoping to never see Iraq again!

Nearly one year after departing my first year in Iraq—I was back again...and not surprisingly, the Iraqi people still needed our help in a big way.

The situation had not changed, in fact they got worse, in my opinion—the chains of injustice were not loosened; the wicked thrived; tyranny and terror was a way of life; and healing was nowhere in sight.

My mission was different though. I represented the Defense Contract Management Agency (DCMA) and my task was to find unaccounted-for money to give back to the Iraq Provisional Government.

My new office was in Baghdad, located in

Saddam's former palace. The palace was now the most prominent structure in what was dubbed the Green Zone, so named because outside the zone, in the rest of Baghdad—the red zone, one met with an increased risk of violence.

I hired thirteen Iraqi nationals to help me with my mission. These thirteen employees represented the moderate, and the progressive future of their country. College educated, they could speak, read, and write English fluently.

One of them, Amal, also knew Spanish. I used her as my primary translator. Her father, whom I'll call Mr. Ethan Ali, was my age. Amal had a younger sister and an older brother.

Amal was a typical young Iraqi girl entering her 'coming of age' period. The only difference between her and any American college girl, besides the obvious geographical location and language, was that her homeland was invaded by a foreign military.

For the second time in two years, my tour of duty was complete, and I went home... this time to retire. I felt relief after retiring, however, I ended up back in Iraq for a third time with a contractor. Another year in a place full of destruction and fractured economy—not to mention, away from home and family.

I did make it home safely once again, and the transition at home was more challenging than I could imagine, but I won't get into that now. That's for another whole story.

Seven years had passed when I received an

unexpected phone call from a refugee agency. They asked me if I would sponsor Mr. Ethan Ali and his family to come and live in America. After asking the extent of my responsibilities, I agreed.

It was not the first time. My wife and I had one of my former employees from Iraq live with us for several months before her husband was able to come to America. So, agreeing to support Mr. Ali was not a new experience for us.

The day came when I, along with my wife, met Mr. Ali and his family at the airport. He was so happy to see us that he held onto me and cried. A team from the agency was present. With Ethan were his wife and his youngest daughter, who was now nineteen. Absent were his son, who was married with children—who came later with his family, and his oldest daughter, Amal.

I was surprised when I did not see Amal. "Where is Amal?" I asked alarmed. Ethan answered that the authorities would not let her come. I looked at the supporting agency representative and inquired, "You knew about this?"

"No, we were unaware of this situation."

"It can be fixed though, right?" I asked pleadingly.

"We will certainly try our best. We'll look into it immediately."

"Thanks, I'd appreciate that and I'm sure the Ali family would too."

I soon learned the reason for Mr. Ali's decision to leave his homeland was because an anonymous caller threatened his life. In Iraq, one takes this sort of calls seriously. His offense? He associated himself with Americans.

As for the oldest daughter, Amal? For five years, many of us have tried several ways to bring Amal to the US, so that she can re-unite with her family. Perhaps the best way to understand her plight is to hear it from her own words:

"Hello, I am Amal, a thirty-year-old girl living in Baghdad, Iraq. My family left me behind after they fled as refugees for helping American soldiers during the war.

I was not allowed to join them.

On a typical day, I arrive home, lock all the doors and windows, cook dinner, watch TV, and fall asleep. Daylight fades until darkness covers the earth. I sit on the floor in the corner—hidden in shadows. The lights are off... I stay quiet. Such is my life.

One night I woke up terrified! There was heavy knocking on my door, and I didn't know what to do. I kept my lights off and checked my phone to see if I missed a call or a text from my neighbors who always warn me of danger. Nothing.

The knocking continued—heavier than before. I froze with fear. A man's voice demanded, 'Open the door!' I was too terrified to respond. It was 12:30 AM.

Were they the police? The Army? Or terrorists pretending to be army members? I heard the stories about terrorists who came to houses dressed like the army or police. If people opened the door they were not seen again.

The knocking stopped. I kept very still. I could not sleep the rest of the night—the rest of the week, in fact.

It has been five long years since my family was forced to leave me behind. They are in America. I am here—in my own country... living in fear... my eyes filled with tears.

Who will deliver me from the grasp of the bad man? Why do I live like a weed in a desolate land? Will I ever hold my mother again? Will I look into the eyes of my father? Will I share a smile with my sister? Only God knows... only God knows."

UPDATE - 2020

Author's note ~ In December 2019, I received a text message from Amal's father, Mr. Ethan Ali. I was in Tennessee at the time, visiting my parents. The message was: "Good news, Amal got her visa and she will be here around January 2020!" The message was followed by several smiley faced emojis.

"Wow! Praise God!" I responded. "This is fantastic news! Our prayers have been answered. We should celebrate!"

Later, on the 1st of January, I received another text informing me that Amal would be arriving at the Miami International Airport on the 2nd of January, along with her younger sister who traveled back to Iraq to help her. Ethan was nervous because the auto designated to take both girls to the airport originated from the U.S. Embassy, where riots were taking place. He blamed the Iranians for stirring up trouble.

He asked that I would pray for both girls. Of course, I did. The flight from Baghdad would travel to Istanbul, Turkey prior to continuing to Miami.

Another text came from Ethan that was urgent. "God is protecting my daughters. News says that Baghdad International Airport was exposed to rockets and all aviation operations stopped! OMG, OMG!"

"I have been praying earnestly for their safe travel," I added.

"Thank you so much for your prayers. Yes, he answers prayer. Thank you God for your mercy. I could not believe my eyes when I saw the news on Al-Arabiya and A-Hurra Iraq."

The girls were to leave Baghdad on the same day that Iranian General Qassem Soleimani got off a commercial airliner in Baghdad. Unlike the two girls, Soleimani was monitored from the moment he boarded the plane in the Lebanese capital of Beirut and landed in Baghdad.

Even after he landed, his car was monitored by drones circling above in the skies of Iraq. One of them, the MQ-9 (Grim) Reaper was armed with laser-guided Hellfire air-to-surface missiles regularly used in attacks on high-value terrorists. The Reaper had Soleimani in its sights for about 10 minutes before firing on two cars carrying the Iranian commander and other senior leaders.[1]

Amal and her younger sister? They had arrived in Istanbul hours before the attack. They were safe! Days later, on the 4th of January, Amal arrived in Miami along with her sister and was finally able to reunite with her family after six years of being the Girl Alone.

[1] Source is from https://www.msn.com/en-us/news/world/us-reaper-drone-left-soleimani-with-little-chance/ar-BBYFMva

To find out more about Scott Meehan and his books, visit www.indiesunited.net/scott-meehan

NARRATIVE NONFICTION

Open Heart, Open Home

Lisa Orban

When I was 16, I was put into foster care. In fewer than two years I was placed with four different families in three different cities, all at the whim of the state and the courts. It was scary and confusing but most of all, lonely. Being thrust into the home of strangers, expected to adapt and fit in without causing any trouble. Learning new rules, different expectations with each new home, your things stuffed into trash bags with each new move. And all of it completely outside your control.

I arrived at Eula's house 21 days after entering foster care. Following my caseworker up the stairs to enter this newest stranger's house, I didn't know what to expect. My heart raced in my chest as we stood outside her parlor in the hallway waiting to meet my newest "mother." In the house behind me I could hear voices and laughter drifting through the air, and an occasional glimpse of the bodies attached to those voices. Looking around the large house, I thought, maybe I could fit in here.

Knocking on the parlor door, my caseworker entered, leaving me to stand alone while I waited for them to call me in. A short time later, I heard them call to me to join them. I shyly shuffled in, looking down at my shoes, hands fidgeting in front of me. When I heard Eula say, "Look up at me child, let me see you."

Slowly raising my head, I saw Eula for the first time, sitting in her chair, smiling at me. Giving me a nod when our eyes met, she raised her arms and said, "Come here child, it's going to be okay now." I walked into her hug, tears in my eyes, feeling as if I had come home.

Eula loved each of us, all of my foster sisters and I, and we all loved her in return, welcoming us as we arrived on her doorstep like a long-lost daughter. On warm evenings, we would all gather around her outside on the porch and share stories. She would listen to us talk about school, the boys we liked, and our lives in general, smiling indulgently at each of us as we talked. She accepted each of us for who we were, giving us unconditional love, no matter what our situation may have been prior to moving in with her. "A clean slate", she declared to each of us coming into her home. What happened in the past was the past. From here on out, we would only be judged by how we acted now, both privileges and punishments based solely on our present behavior. I loved her dearly for that. I think everyone in her home did.

Sadly, I was only allowed to stay with her for four months before being moved again, to another city, with another family. None as warm or as loving as what I had had with her. But while I was with her, she taught me to accept people as they were and to never hold their past against them, to take in those in need of help and to love them while they were with me. I have carried those lessons with me for the rest of my life.

I now own a large house of my own, often filled to capacity (and sometimes beyond) with people who need a second chance. It started slowly, more by accident than design; a 17-year-old girl whose parents had chosen drugs over her. Then a 17-year-old boy who had been thrown out of a religious sect, left sitting at a gas station, all of his belongings stuffed into garbage bags. Then two young men, one recently released from the Army who had lost their apartment. From there, it snowballed.

Each person who left would be replaced by someone else, brought to me by someone I had helped before. They come to me broke, desperate, often scared, and with nowhere else to go. They come to me because the system we live in is broken, without adequate safety nets, and very little compassion. They come to me because they need a second chance, a hand up when the world has pushed them down. They come to me, because they have no place in our society, but desperately want to have one.

I have for the last ten years now taken in hundreds of people. I have taken in pregnant women who, when they could no longer work, lost their homes because there is no paid medical or family leave in our country. I have taken in ex-vets who, after going to war, find it difficult to readjust to civilian life and find our country has forgotten their service as soon as they took off their uniforms. I have taken in ex-cons who cannot find work or a place to live because they made a mistake, a mistake more often stemming from poverty and desperation, rather than any true malicious intent. I have taken in families when one of the parents has lost their minimum-wage job and they could no longer afford to live on their own. I have taken in all those that society has washed their hands of or simply looked away saying, "It's not our problem." The ones that fall through the cracks of our fractured society.

I often laugh and say that I'm running a flophouse, but it's not that well organized. It is not run as a shelter; it is my home, and while they are with me it is their home too. Each person treated as family, free to come and go as they please, safely secure in the knowledge that there is someone who cares about them as they put their lives back together. There are very few rules in my house. Only two really: help when you can and respect the people around you. My house is often filled with laughter, music, and chaos, each person adding to the tapestry of our lives here, making it a vibrant place to live. I have had artists, musicians, fire spinners, poets, and painters, and a variety of other characters have graced my doorstep over the years. They stay with me for a while. There is no time limit, only when they are ready do they move on. Stepping out of my house with confidence that they can make it on their own, to scatter across the city, and the country, some as far away as Alaska and Hawaii.

In all my years of doing this and all the hundreds of people I have helped, only twice have I had a problem with someone who, with regret, I had to remove from my home. The most common problem I have is simply that there is only one bathroom for sometimes upwards of twelve people. I dream of the day I will have enough money to put in a second bathroom, but until then we cope as best we can, while waiting for our turn. We share what we have, help each other out, support each other when things are bad, and celebrate with them when things are good. Each new person learning what it is to belong to a family again, or maybe even for the first time.

I give each of them my unconditional love, I accept who they are without reservation, and I give each of them a clean slate as they walk through my door. Everyone deserves a second chance to get it right, to learn from their mistakes without paying for them for the rest of their lives. To learn how to stand up proudly and feel worthy of being treated like a person, someone who matters, maybe for the first time in their lives.

I have made a difference. I cannot change the world, but I can change the world for one person, and for me, right now, that is enough.

To find out more about Lisa Orban and her books, visit
www.indiesunited.net/lisa-orban

NARRATIVE FICTION

Pollination

Aaron S Gallagher

"I'm sorry to bother you," he said, "but you have very kind eyes."

T*hat's a new one,* she thought. "Oh?"

"Yes. I wanted to tell you that. Would you like to have a coffee with me?" He had an affable smile, tousled short brown hair, and remote but kind green eyes.

She smiled, touched her curly black hair at the nape of her neck, but said, "I'm meeting friends."

"Certainly. Of course. I could help you wait," he offered. She looked him up and down. He held out a hand; it was clean and his nails were in good order. "I'm Michael."

She took his hand and shook with him. "Margie."

"Lovely to meet you, Miss..." he trailed off with raised eyebrows.

She grinned. "Baldwin," she consented. "Margie Baldwin. Smooth."

"Lovely to meet you, Ms. Baldwin. I'm Michael Hancock. Would you like to sit with me?" he gestured to the table in front of the coffee shop. Around them, London bustled by. "We could watch for your friends."

"I guess so," she said. He held her chair out for her, a gesture she wasn't accustomed to. He even pushed it in. He sat across from her and raised a hand to the waiter. After they ordered, he said, "Friends?"

"Pardon?"

"You said waiting for friends. Not a boyfriend or a husband? A woman with eyes like yours, I find it impossible to believe."

She arched one eyebrow. "To the point, aren't you?"

His face showed good humor, and he said, "Merely asking. Not asking."

She narrowed her eyes. "That's a line if I've ever heard one."

"Not really," he said. "Promise."

Their coffee arrived, and they went through the customizations. After a sip, she said, "And you? No girlfriend or wife?"

His face seemed remote. "No," he said.

She pointed at the ring on his finger. He didn't try to hide it or look guilty about it. He touched it with his thumb, a movement that seemed practiced. "Not anymore," he amended.

"Turn you in on a new model?" she asked. "Or was it you that traded up?"

"Neither," he said. He took a deep breath. "I had two perfect years. Two perfectly perfect years. And then two that weren't so perfect. And now that's over."

She frowned. "What happened?"

"What do you do?" he asked.

"I'm a secretary."

"No," he corrected with a grin, "that's your job. What do you *do*?"

She half-smiled. "I paint."

"What do you paint, Margie Baldwin?"

"Watercolors. Landscapes," she conceded as if confessing. "I like to paint landscapes."

He nodded. "Joanna was a physicist."

"Joanna?"

His face became reverent. "Joanna Marie Dellacorte Hancock," he said carefully and his eyes brightened. "My wife. She was a physicist. It was what she did *and* what she did. She loved her work. Loved her job. She was going to make the world better. Safer."

"What happened?"

"She was young. Young and full of life and hope and dreams… and willing to believe her employer when they made assurances about such things as safety precautions and equipment."

She swallowed. "But what happened?"

"Cancer," he said.

"Oh. I'm sorry. Er, what sort of cancer, if I may ask?"

He gave her a tired, gentle smile. "All of them, I think."

She sighed and said nothing. They sipped their coffee as the moment passed.

"What do you do, Michael?"

His smile elevated several notches "I travel."

"Travel?"

"Yes. You see, one night over a gourmet dinner of grilled cheese and tomato soup Joanna and I made a list of places we thought we would like to see together. And since you don't have to budget a dream, we thought *big*. When everything was over and her employer was forced to admit that perhaps their safety precautions had been lacking, I found I had the means. And so I travel. Every place on our list," he said.

"Oh," she smiled. "How many places have you been?"

"All of them," he told her.

"You just travel?"

"I travel. I went to every place on that list. And when I got there, I found a person with kind eyes. Eyes like yours. Eyes like *hers*. And I told them her story. I told them her name. And so, there are hundreds of people out there in the world who know who she was. Who know her name. Just as you do."

She swallowed the lump in her throat. "That's lovely," she said.

He nodded. He checked his watch and said, "It's time to go. You're waiting on friends."

"It's okay," she said. "You don't have to go."

"I do," he assured her.

"Where are you going next?"

He stood, took several bills from his wallet, and laid them on the table. "It was lovely to meet you, Ms. Baldwin. *Thank you.* Thank you for coffee, and for talking with me."

"Where are you going next?" she asked again, rising with him.

He put his hands in his pockets. "Good evening," he said. With a slight bow, he turned and walked down the street, blending into the crowd. And he was gone.

She sat, staring at the place where he had vanished. She sat there until her friends found her. They sat. "Hello," Kate said, waving a hand. "Earth to Margie. Earth to Margie. Come in, Margie."

Margie blinked at Kate and Della. "Oh. Hi."

"Where were you?" Della asked.

"Hmm? Oh," Margie mused, frowning, "there was- there was a man…"

"OoooOOOH," Kate cooed. "A maaayun."

"It's not like that," Margie insisted. She considered. "He was married."

"Margie!" Della scolded.

"No, no," Margie said. "It was… he was…"

She stared into the crowd, searching. "Her name," she said, "was Joanna. Joanna Marie Dellacorte Hancock. And she was a physicist…"

To find out more about Aaron S Gallagher and his books, visit
www.indiesunited.net/aaron-gallagher

COMING OF AGE

Unbuttoned

Timothy R. Baldwin

I don't remember when I first saw her. Perhaps it was from afar as I watched her play on the soccer field. Maybe it wasn't. But I was smitten the moment her features met my eyes. She was cuter and far less sexy back then. Her curves still showed despite the loose track pants and t-shirts she wore every day. Her outfits had very little variety. I think that's what first drew me to her. Her apparent simplicity.

Impossibly infatuated, I was incapacitated.

You know the feeling. When you've been so enthralled by someone that what holds you back, what keeps you from talking to that person is sheer terror. Terror at tumbling over your words, at suddenly having nothing to say, or even worse. Committing to a date only to find yourself staring at her from across the table with absolutely nothing to say and still several hours before the date is over.

I first met Michelle. Truly met her, I mean. And not just stared at her from the sidelines or talked to her on the phone after finding out her name and working up the nerve to call her.

It was at Bible Club that we first met, and I wasn't sure if she knew that I was the guy who called her up while she so graciously talked and listened for hours.

But she knew.

I could tell when she came to me and smiled. She was radiant. Her teeth seemed to show whiter and brighter beneath the classroom's fluorescent lights. Her skin, a light brown, blushed. She said hello and barely looked me in the eye. I stammered a hello back to her. We talked for about a minute, skirting around what we both knew to be truly weird — me getting her number without asking for it and calling her, even though we'd never really met in person.

Maybe she found me in the school yearbook.

Like I found her.

At Bible Club she got in front of the group and gave her testimony, citing some scripture verses meaningful to her. I wasn't listening. But I knew then that I wanted to somehow be a better person. To be someone she would admire as I admired her. For her looks, yes. But also, for her kindness and the way she wore a smile and carried herself, inviting everyone into her world.

She was attractive then. She didn't know it. Or, perhaps her Protestant morality refrained her from flaunting it. I don't know because I never got a date with her in the ninth grade.

Oh, I'd sit with her at lunch.

A few seats away.

With my band of buddies.

At another table.

I'd look up at her and see her between rolling hills of heads and shoulders that slanted daintily to allow me to catch a glimpse of her as she ate and chatted with her friends.

My buddies, Stephen and Matt. They'd catch me looking at Michelle. One would glance over his shoulder, then back at me. Then, the other would mimic my expression and toss something at my face. Maybe a cold, soggy tater tot would hit its mark, and Michelle's spell on me would momentarily be broken. I'd come back to my buddies, and they would laugh.

Behind them, nearly back to back to Stephen and Matt, would be Michelle's friends Eve and Clarisse. Like Stephen and Matt, they were probably staring at Michelle, who'd catch my eye and smile. I'd smile back, which I think gave my friends the perfect opportunity to toss a particle of poorly prepared food in my face. Michelle would cover her mouth with the tips of her fingers, stifling a laugh as her cheeks dimpled and blushed. Eve and Clarisse would glance back at me. And they would roll their eyes.

No matter.

I once worked up the nerve to ask her out.

But I blew it.

I created the moment for casual conversation with Eve and Clarisse when Michelle was not around. Easy to do since they took some honors classes with me while Michelle took, as I would later find out, pretty much all AP courses.

The goal of these conversations was information. I was finding out about Michelle without actually getting to know her. We've all been there, and for me, it was a need. I needed to find that common ground before committing to hours with someone I hardly knew.

She liked the same band as me.

I told her I had two tickets to the show happening that weekend.

"Do you want to come?" I asked.

"Of course," she exclaimed, "that would be awesome!"

So, we had a date, except for one technicality. Did you know that it is not a date if you do not say 'date' or definitively state 'do you want to go out with me'?

So, there I was — nauseated with nervousness — and that one simple four-letter word doesn't come out. Instead, it's just an invitation from a friend.

Or acquaintances.

Or strangers.

Two people with endless potential as long as one of them doesn't steer the relationship in the wrong direction or propel it forward too quickly.

"Great," I said as I fought back nausea. "I'll pick you up at your place."

"All right," she said and began to walk with me.

Most guys would be elated by this.

Most guys would even be bold enough to take the girl's hand, or maybe put an arm around her waist.

I'm not most guys.

I don't even know what her reaction was when I began to pick up speed. I have a faint memory of her walking beside me and trying to keep up. Maybe she asked if I was okay. But I lost her as I darted into the boy's bathroom and found the last stall. I knelt, taking deep breaths and swallowing until my stomach stopped fluttering.

When I came out of the bathroom, she was gone.

When I saw her again, I didn't bring up the incident.

Neither did she.

She was kind and gracious.

Me, I couldn't wait for our "date."

Here's the thing. There's dating: a guy asks a girl out. Or vice versa. But it's almost always better when the guy asks the question. After that, the girl can say yes or no. It's official and clearly communicates the intention of both parties. Then, they go out. In high school, it's always a little weird, especially if you don't have a car.

"Hey, so, I'll pick you up at 7," you say.

"Great," she says.

Then, you arrive. Your date is all dressed up and smells of strawberries and vanilla. The girl smiles at you, and you smile at her, except you're not really looking at her face. You're looking at her cleavage. She notices but doesn't say anything. You bring your eyes up to meet hers. Then, you take her hand in yours and walk her to the car.

Well, your parent's car. A ten-year-old maroon station wagon with some rust around the wheel wells. And this would be all fine and good except that your mom is driving.

Or maybe your dad.

I'm not sure which is worse.

For you, it might be your mom.

For me, it would be my dad. He'd say something weird that would make your date really uncomfortable. Then, the two of you would be sitting in the backseat and looking at each other in absolute silence.

You'd wear that expression that says, *I swear I have nothing to do with this.*

She'd wear that expression that says, *Oh, jeez, I'm going out with a loser who doesn't even have his license.*

And your dad would be sharing these corny jokes and telling these stories about his first date.

And she'd laugh. Not the mocking kind, but the kind that lets you know she's just pleased to be with you. She doesn't think you're a loser. Also, she finds your dad kind of adorable.

At least, that's what Michelle told me when my dad dropped us off at the arena where the band was playing.

"You know," Michelle said as we started to walk, "your dad's kind of cute in that dad sort of way."

"Okay," I said. "Uh… thanks."

She chuckled. "I can see where you get it from." Then, she took my hand and pushed against me a little as we walked.

Silently, I thanked my dad for being my unlikely wingman.

I pulled her closer to me. As close as she could be without knocking me off balance. And we walked like that until we reached the line and she spotted someone she knew. She squealed the way girls sometimes do when they are excited, with the entirety of emotion, shooting like rays of electricity out of her extended fingers. She took off like a rocket.

I thought she was running toward a group of girls, but she passed them as though they didn't exist and ran up to a guy who caught her in his arms and squeezed her one of those big bear hugs. When I caught up to them, he was gently setting her down. Then she, on tiptoes, was giving him a peck on the cheek.

I don't think she saw me.

Or maybe she just didn't notice me on purpose.

Like a puppy placed out in the rain after piddling on the floor, I stood there and waited awkwardly as Michelle and this other guy engaged in a little catching up. It wasn't clear if they'd dated previously. It also wasn't clear whether they were just super friendly with each other, or whether she just greeted everyone with a 'Holy Kiss.'

Fuck if I knew. This was my first time seeing Michelle outside school.

"Oh, Brian," Michelle said at last as if I had just arrived. "This is Gabe."

"Hey," I said as I took his hand. "How long have you known each other?"

"Oh," Gabe said with eyes that seemed to look past you when he talked. "We kind of grew up together. Michelle's older brother is my best friend."

"Cool," I said, nodding politely as if his response explained everything I needed to know about the history of their relationship.

Meanwhile, Gabe droned on uninterestingly

about the older brother I did not know Michelle had. And all his incessant talking did for me was raise more questions. I wondered whether this older brother was also at our high school. If so, should I try to get on this guy's good side? You know, score some points with him and impress little sis. None of these unasked questions were answered by Gabe's monologue.

"Anyway," Gabe said at last with an ambiguous wink." You two enjoy the show. I gotta catch up with my girl."

"My brother," Michelle said as she turned to me. "He's a senior."

It was a moment before I registered what Michelle was referring to. I was still trying to catch my breath over the knowledge that Gabe would simply not be a contender for Michelle's heart.

"Oh," I said dumbly. Then I cleared my throat and added. "My sister's a senior, too."

"Yeah, I know," Michelle said. "We play on the soccer team together. You know, the team you watch when you should be practicing on your field. Anyway, she's… uh… mentioned you before."

"Like what did she say?" I asked, trying to mask my surprise.

Her hazel eyes sparkled. "Like you're a little weird," she said. "Maybe you read too much. But don't worry, I'm a little weird, too. At least that's what my brother says."

We forced a laugh. Mine went on a little longer than hers. She squinted at me as if to say, *the joke's over.*

"Sorry," I said.

"It's okay," Michelle said. She bumped her hip against mine and knocked me off balance. "Happens to the best of us."

We stood in line. Michelle started in on a story of sibling rivalry. I added a similar story when she'd finished. Together, we were enjoying the sweet, safe comfort of friendship. As we talked, we moved forward in the line, getting close enough to each other to rub shoulders. Just close enough to make it easy for me to casually place my arm around her waist. I took a risk, albeit a small one, in hopes that she would return the gesture.

And she did. Her arm was upon my back, and her hand was around my waist. Side by side, we pressed against each other, and the curve of her hip up to the curve of her breast resonated warmth. My heart raced, pumping the heat of longing and desire simultaneously to my groin and to my head.

Then we separated at the ticket booth where I fumbled with my wallet before handing the agent some cash.

"Don't you already have tickets?" Michelle asked.

"I did," I said and fumbled with the rest of my explanation.

Michelle nodded knowingly.

And that night, her physical absence at my side where she had pressed against me for the span of maybe five minutes cooled the heat of my desire. If I'd planned it better, perhaps the night would have ended differently.

Perhaps not.

Nonetheless, we enjoyed the potential of whatever we would be — friends, lovers, gentle companions, the pleasure of our company, or just ships in the night signaling their presence to each other with the flash of lights and the blare of a horn.

In our enjoyment, we watched the show, occasionally stealing a glance at the intriguing mystery who stood to our right or left respectively while the other pretended not to notice.

For two years, I sputtered along in Michelle's wake. I'd steal a glance at her, she'd return my gaze with a smile as she sailed on with a group of her friends. When she'd disappear over the horizon, I'd allow the tide to take me to my next class.

That is, until one afternoon, I was running late. I'd decided upon a shortcut and slammed the release bar to a door that led to a stairwell. It opened to the then unfamiliar sounds of show-tunes.

Michelle and her best friends, Eve and Clarisse, sat on the steps. Their voices were harmonizing, taking full advantage of the acoustics. I tried to walk past them. But a tug at my pant leg held me fast.

"Brian," Michelle sang. "We need a 'Melchior,'" Eve and Clarisse repeated her, as if in a refrain.

"A what?" I asked. I had no idea what she meant. She'd always been a great singer, and we hadn't been hanging out since she'd join the drama club.

In unison, the three of them told me it was for *Spring Awakening*. I still had no idea what the trio meant.

"The musical," they sang. Hot and flirty, chatting

in some code known only to themselves, the trio whispered about how perfect I would be.

"Brian," they said. "Sing for us."

So, I did, and my voice cracked until Michelle smiled at me. Two dimpled cheeks the color of sweet hot cocoa warmed me up to the idea of performing in her show. Though I never sang publicly, I did for her. What guy wouldn't? What with the cute way her smile perked up her cheeks until her hazel eyes sparkled with a wink. Oh, and her boobs that ballooned just slightly out of her tight gingham pattern shirt begging to be unbuttoned.

Boy, had she grown.

I was snagged like a ship run aground on a coral reef.

Caught in the throes of raging hormones that overcame any sense I had — I had none. If I did, I would have hoisted my sails and retreated like an outgunned ship until the predatory danger of involving myself with a girl I now knew was way above my league found some other hapless victim. But, like most theatre girls in high school, she had about her an intriguing mystery magnified by every too-tight-in-just-the right-places outfits she wore. They were tight enough to cause a guy to stumble up steps as he did a double-take. He'd watch her descend a crowded stairwell between classes. That's when she'd glance over her shoulder and flash the guy a rosy smile.

Yeah, it was definitely her smile that had me.

"Brian," Michelle sang sweetly. "Come perform in our play."

"I don't know, maybe," I told her.

"But you'll be great," Eve and Clarisse chimed in, adding some mindless laughter of their own.

"When?" I asked them.

"Here," Michelle said. She stood up with a bounce and waved a form in front of me.

Being just out of my reach, I stepped closer the way sailors hypnotized by the siren's song sail closer to land until they shipwreck. Even then, they don't realize it. Neither did I, not with the scent of strawberries and vanilla wafting toward me, drawing me closer until I landed upon her island and I was trapped.

So, yeah. I unbuttoned her…

Curiosity.

And she led me down territory that my seventeen years would have never led me on their own. We performed. On stage, that is. And we became that weird mismatched theatre couple. Me, the guy who grew to the underwhelming height of 5-foot-9. She, the girl whose bosoms blossomed beyond a B in middle school and surpassed a D in high school. I'm guessing, though. I never bothered to understand bra sizes. But, still, you get the point.

And the point is this. A girl's charming smile and her self-confidence will get a guy to do just about anything.

To find out more about Timothy R. Baldwin and his books, visit www.indiesunited.net/timothy-baldwin

Summer

HUMOROUS NONFICTION

Everyone Needs a Jim

Lisa Orban

Over the years my children have said things that made me stop, drop, and laugh more than once from little innocuous things to huge whoppers of misunderstanding. Their innocent misconceptions of the world have had me laughing so hard I've had tears run from my eye. When listening to a child talk about how the world works gives you an interesting view of your life as seen by their guileless eyes. The insights and perceptions of how or why things are, is often oddly skewed, as if they are peeping into the adult world through carnival mirrors. There are many such family stories, often told and retold at gatherings with gusto, the following story is one of our favorites, so please, sit back and enjoy this brief glimpse into my life.

When my children were young, my friend Jim would come to visit whenever he was in town and over the years it slowly morphed into dedicated weekly visits. Every weekend, Jim would arrive to a loud and enthusiastic welcome by my children, each one excited to share their week with him; from homework to hobbies he listened attentively, nodding and responding in all the right places. He'd bring games to play with them that he thought they'd enjoy, and introduced them to his favorite comics and cartoons. He'd tell them stories and sing, badly, I might add, to them to keep them distracted while I made dinner and at the end of the day, he'd help me get them ready for bed after an exciting day of play with their favorite person.

Some weekends he would help me with some project around the house or the yard. And at other times, when the children had been especially good or we had something special to celebrate, he would take all of us out to dinner. Other times, after getting the kids to bed, I would have a sitter come over so that just the two of us could get away for a while and to enjoy a night out without children. It was a routine we all enjoyed, and after a week of mommy duty it was always a welcome reprieve to talk about movies that didn't involve a cartoon character, books without brightly colored pictures, or artwork that didn't come from my children. He was a wonderful friend to the whole family and we all enjoyed his visits.

This was just part of our routine of life, and I thought very little of it until one day I received a phone from Néa, a good friend who also operated the daycare my children attended. When she was able to stop laughing long enough to make full sentences, this was the story she relayed to me.

My oldest daughter, then 8, was in the car with Néa as they were on their way home from the park for lunch. When they stopped at an intersection waiting for the light to turn green, my daughter noticed they were in front of her favorite restaurant, the Chinese buffet. From the back seat she piped up excitedly and said, "Can we eat there today?"

Néa turned to see where she was pointing, and shook her head at the request, "No honey, not today."

Disappointed, my daughter asked, "Why not?"

"Well," said Néa, "I just don't have enough money right now to take everyone out to lunch today." Thinking this was the end of it, she continued to drive now that the light had turned green.

My daughter was quiet for a block or two and then said, "Néa, you need a Jim just like my Mommy has!"

Startled speechless for a moment, she quickly regained her composure, asked, "What do you mean honey?"

With great authority on the subject, my daughter informed her, "Well, my Mommy has a Jim and he takes her out for dinner and plays with us and sometimes he even takes us out for dinner when we're good, and I've been very good today. And Jims always have money to do fun things. You don't have any money, so you need a Jim too."

Laughing, Néa told her, "Honey, not everybody has a Jim like your Mommy does."

My daughter was quiet processing this information until they were almost in front of Néa's house. "Néa," my daughter sighed with exasperation, "*everybody* needs a Jim!"

And you know, when you put it like that, I couldn't disagree, everyone does need a Jim.

To find out more about Lisa Orban and her books,
visit
www.indiesunited.net/lisa-orban

PARANORMAL HORROR

The Island of Babushkas

Muhammad Idrees

Lorenzo awoke and found himself under a tall tree. There was a dead silence and all he could see was the crystal blue water in front of him and a thick jungle of trees behind him. Nervous and horrified, he did not know where he was or how he came to that strange place. After piecing together recent events, he remembered he had come along with his three friends to spend his weekend on the island.

There was a small hut he had made with his friends out of bamboos and a thick thatch of straw. They had also brought chairs and tables.

The evening before, he and his friends had drunk a lot and then he heard the flute music so pleasant and magical he followed it, leaving his drunk friends behind. That was all he could remember.

Pushing himself up from the tree, he decided he needed to find a way out of this place. First, he walked along the beach for some time, but he felt like he had been walking on the same track again and again. Changing course, he went through the shadow of the dense jungle, followed by the steep craggy rocks. After covering miles of distance, he felt tired but still could not find any clue to a way out.

"It seems a very strange island," he said to himself. He climbed up a hill, hoping to find a possible way out. He was nervous this would be where he would spend his night, it was getting dark and he was completely lost.

From the top of the hill, he saw a house with lights on giving him hope for survival. He descended the hill and sped towards the house.

He knocked on the door, and an old woman answered.

"I came to the island with my friends but…"

Interrupting him, the old woman said indifferently, "Come in."

It was a small hall with a long wooden table in the middle, having chairs all around. On the walls, there were portraits of old ladies with scarves on their heads, giving them the look of Russian *babushkas*. There was another old lady cleaning the glass of the window. The table and chair were clean, though old and worn out. Lorenzo sat in the middle of the table, embarrassed and puzzled. He again heard the flute music from the inside of the house followed by the voices of several ladies singing a song he had not heard before. While he listened to the music, another old woman brought in a bowl of soup along with some empty plates. He noticed the women were all of the same age, and even resembled one another so much that one would not think they were different women. Even the photos on the wall resembled one another, only the color of the scarves varied.

Lorenzo was hungry and turning his attention to the bowl he started on the soup. The old woman who had brought him the soup looked at him in utter embarrassment and walked away. After drinking half the bowl, he felt a hard object at the bottom. Lorenzo was astonished to discover two human fingers floating to the surface. He felt vomit rise in his throat. He looked around to complain but saw none of the old women. He stood, took the bowl and moved towards the inside.

The first door from the lounge was the kitchen. "Hello? Hello, is anybody there? I have something very strange and unusual in my soup… it looks like human fingers… or maybe something… anybody there?"

There was no one in the kitchen, so he moved to the next room, from which the sound of music came. The door was open and he saw seven or eight old women busy in different types of work. One was stirring a spatula in a big black cauldron; smoke rolled out, revealing something was boiling. Some were cleaning the dishes, at a table two others were cutting up human organs. Horrified, the bowl of soup fell down from his hands, shattering as it hit the floor. The sound alerted the old women to his presence.

He turned and ran toward the main door. But as he reached the door an old woman stood in his way, holding an axe. He pushed her away but two others pulled at his shirt from behind and he fell to the floor. When they reached for him, he snatched fistfuls of their hair and struck their heads together. Scrambling back to the door, he reached for the doorknob but the old woman with the axe struck at him, the axe biting into his left hand. Punching her in face with his other hand, he managed to open the door and escape. His hand bled freely as he ran blindly as fast as he could.

But they did not chase him. The house was their barrier, it was as far as they could go. "You are very lucky that you escaped," he heard whispered into his ear as he ran. "No one has ever escaped here alive before you. People come here of their own free will but do not leave that way. You are lucky…"

Holding his hand tightly to his chest to stop the flow of blood, the words slipped from his ears the further he ran. Some distance away he stumbled and fell to the ground, slipping into unconsciousness.

Regaining consciousness the following day, he found himself in a hospital room.

Seeing him awake, the doctor smiled and said, "I am very glad that your friends and the rescue team were able to find you and bring you to the hospital. But I am very sorry, we had to remove two of your fingers due to the severity of your injuries." Unwrapping the object he had held in his hand, the doctor reveled Lorenzo's two missing fingers.

They were the same ones he had seen floating in his soup.

To find out more about Muhammand Idrees and his books, visit
www.indiesunited.net/muhammand-idrees

FICTION

Jeeves

Ketan Desai

When confronted with an epidemic, I thought, why not turn to that epitome of unflappable knowledge, Jeeves, for a story? And being a medic, clinical problem had to be thrown in. To complete the dish, I added in British humor. And voila, there was a story on Jeeves in the era of COVID19.

"What ho, Jeeves", I said. "What ho, what ho, what ho!' The last one just in case the previous ones had not quite made the point.

"Warm felicitations to you as well, Sir."

"Well, whaho!"

"As you say, Sir, whaho indeed."

Having dispensed with the necessary formalities, it was time to move the conversation along. "So, you wanted to see me?" It's not too often that Jeeves wanted to see me. But the poor man must have finally come to his senses and realize the genius of Bertram Wooster. We Woosters are known for our great minds.

The bloke was clearly vexed. His upper lip even

quivered a bit.

"Yes, sir. It is a matter of some delicacy".

Delicacy usually meant only one thing- Anatole was going to go on a culinary rampage. But that could not be it, as the poor chap was stuck in France with some virus or horrible little pestilence. So, no French cuisine extravaganza. The alternatives were frightening.

"Is it Aunt Agatha? Has she found a way to hitch me to Madeline again? Good heavens, man, that is not a matter of delicacy! That is a national emergency, to be handled on a war footing".

"No, Sir. Lady Gregson is quarantined in her castle and has had little time to attend to your marital status, distressing as it is for her".

"Well, then what? Has good old Augustus Fink Nottle been thrown out of the Drone's club? Or has Honoria Glossop tied the knot with Bingo Little? That is not a matter of delicacy! That is worth celebrating!" It would get Honoria out of my life, and ground Bingo, and nothing could be better than that. Even I got tired of bailing Bingo out of the pokey.

"No sir, none of those probabilities have come to pass."

"Well then, man, what is it? Spit it out! Don't just stand there like a fish, opening and closing your mouth."

"It has to do with your, um, bowel habits, Sir."

"My bowel habits? There is nothing wrong with my habits. Everything is as habitual as they are supposed to be," I sniffed. The arrogance of the man. There are some things an Englishman doesn't talk about, even with his manservant. The nerve of him to bring that up!

"Well, sir, it wasn't so much as the habits, it was what was in them that was of some concern."

That was too much. Is there no privacy or sanctity in an English home anymore?

"I say, old chap, have you been poking into the loo?" It was as I feared. After all these years of service, he had finally cracked. It was time for a manly talk. "Take a holiday Jeeves. This moment of madness will pass."

"No, sir, I have not been poking, as you so succinctly put it, in the loo. But I did notice a stain in your trousers from last night."

He was right. This was rather delicate.

"Well, it was the Indian takeout we got last night. It was a little hot, if you know what I mean."

"Maybe, sir, but the color was red, so it could not have been the takeout."

"The takeout had chilies, and those are red, so it has to be those. Jeeves, that is all there is to it. Let's not talk about this silliness anymore!"

"Unfortunately, Sir, it has to be addressed. Your monthly allowance mandates that all health-related issues be handled promptly".

"Dash it, Jeeves, I can't do anything right now. All doctors' offices are closed. Besides, no one needs to know, right?" I winked,

"I believe I can take care of the matter, sir!" Excellent. He was seeing it my way, bending to the superior will of the Woosters. He disappeared in the wink of the eye, coattails and all, only to appear a moment later. Under his arms was a box of gloves and a jar of petrolatum jelly.

"Good heavens, Jeeves, you can't be serious! This is completely ridiculous! You have no medical training!"

"I'll have you know, sir, that my cousin Archibald, thrice removed on my mother's side, was a paramedic during the war!"

"You are not Archibald, Jeeves! Let him come and examine!" That would put things off till I thought a decent way out of this.

"Unfortunately, cousin Archibald is no longer amongst us. He was run over by an Indian take-out a few months ago. But he did impart a significant amount of training to me, which I studied assiduously. I am quite competent to evaluate the matter at hand and report accordingly to Lady Gregson. I'm sure my report will permit continued issue of those monthly cheques."

Well, he had me over a barrel. Gosh darn it, it was either get examined or it was toodle-oo and pip-pip to the allowance.

"Ok Jeeves, go ahead".

As I unbuckled my belt, I glanced at Jeeves. His face was impassive as ever, but I could have sworn there was a hint of smile on those lips. And a glint in his eyes.

To find more about Ketan Desai and his books, visit
www.indiesunited.net/ketan-desai

SCIENCE FICTION

My Summer Job

Ralph Rotten

I knew right away there was something strange about that carnival.

The year was 1966, and I was a skinny young graduate student at the University of Illinois. My folks used to grind me every year to get a summer job. Mom said it would build character, and Dad said that it was the least I could do if I wasn't going to join the Marines and serve my country like my cousin was doing. But there was no way on Earth was I going to join the war machine in Viet Nam. I'd protested against the war three times. Of course, I sure as hell wasn't going to tell my Dad about the protests; that was a good way to get a knuckle sandwich and a boot in the ass. So every year I compromised and found a summer job. The last three years I'd managed to pick up part-time work with the carnivals that would set up shop every year down on Route 66.

It was a perfect gig, really. The carnival would be in town for a few weeks, so I could earn some beer money and get Dad off my ass. After the carnival moved on, I'd tell my folks I couldn't find anything else and spend the rest of the summer hanging out with my friends.

But there was actually more to it than that. See, I was a sociology student back then, working on my PHD in behavioral sciences, and somehow, I found it fascinating to study the carnies who ran the show. I know it sounds snooty, but carnies are an odd breed of humans. For me it was like travelling back in time and observing *homus erectus* or *homus habilis*. These were people who were one step above homeless. They were the unwashed, uneducated masses. With my long hippy hair and a goatee I could almost blend in amongst them, *at least as long as I kept my mouth shut*. Working in a carnival afforded me a great chance to study these lower life forms up close and personal.

But this year there was just something different about the carnival. At first it was the little things that seemed out of place, like their prices. See, the primary purpose of a carnival midway is to separate patrons from their cash. Normally they use all sorts of scams like ticket books that only contained a few tickets for the really cool rides so you had to keep buying more ticket books. Then there were the rigged games that were impossible to win, or the over-priced food. In short, even though they were a step above cavemen, carnies were quite devious at their graft.

But not this place. Nope! You paid one low price for a little bracelet that let you ride as many attractions as you wanted to. Not only that, but the games were actually winnable... and it seemed like everyone was carrying around big stuffed animals they'd won for their girlfriend. Cotton candy was a dime, and you could stuff yourself with hot dogs and candy apples for a buck. Right away I was suspicious; *how could they possibly be making a profit?*

But that wasn't the end of it. There was something about the carnies, like they all had these dead eyes. No one ever smiled, and whenever I approached a group of them, they'd all stop talking... if you could call what they were doing talking. They'd just lean in close to each other like they were about to say something, but their mouths wouldn't move at all. I mean, they could talk, I'd heard them speak whenever they sent me on a new task. But when they were talking to each other it was always that weird, wordless, joining of the heads.

The strangest of them all was L. Urch. At least that was the name stenciled on his coveralls. He was this big, tall, goony guy who ran the haunted house and was always looming over me whenever I worked there. He had those same dead eyes as the rest of them, like he had risen from the grave or something. Honestly, I think he was scarier than the ride itself.

And then there was Skip and Gill, the guys who ran Gravitron. Skip was the fat one, and Gill was the short one that always seemed to be hunched over. Actually, the full name stenciled on Skip's name tag was Skip R. Gill's nametag read Gill E. Gann. Anyone living in 1966 would have made the immediate connection to the Skipper and Gilligan. I always figured their names were just too much of a coincidence and that they were really fugitives living under assumed names. But what kind of moron would choose names from Gilligan's Island, right? They were super creepy. Although they were almost always together, I never saw them speak a single word to one another. Skip would just kind of look at Gill with those dead eyes, and off would go Gilligan… I mean Gill, to do his bidding. Not only that, but Skip was always watching me. I'd turn around and there he was staring at me like one of those paintings where the eyes followed you wherever you went.

Miss Endora ran the place, and yes, she was a witch. I don't mean like she had magical powers like the Endora on Bewitched, but she was mean as hell. She'd sit in her little ticket booth and yell angry directions at the summer help like me. She was the only one that didn't have dead eyes. In fact, she had mean eyes. Like, if looks could kill, that lady could have murdered the entire staff with a single glance. Even the regulars seemed like they were afraid of her. She'd give them one of her evil stares and off they'd go to do whatever she'd wordlessly told them to do. It was downright unnerving.

Like I said, the whole place just seemed off somehow. I wanted to tell my friends about it, but what could I say? *Oh, they're suspicious because their prices are entirely affordable*? If I said anything, my friends would laugh and say it was just me reading too many books. And it was true; every minute of free time I had my face in a book. I'd just finished reading Heinlein's *Stranger in a Strange Land*, and was a huge fan of Ray Bradbury ever since

I read *A Sound of Thunder* the previous summer. Maybe they were right, and this was all just my imagination.

It was a week into the job when things finally came to a head. I'd managed to score a nickel-bag of Acapulco Gold with my first paycheck, and back then all the best stuff came from Mexico. I didn't dare leave my stash at home for fear of having my Dad find it. Not only would he beat me with a stick (literally), but they would probably kick me out of the house. In 1966 it was a big deal to get caught smoking pot.

So there I am on my dinner break, hiding over between the trailers where the carnies all lived. It was downwind from the big concession stand so the smell of the deep-fryer covered the stench of the weed. I was crouched in the dark doing my best to pick out all of the seeds before I rolled a doobie. It was a perfect spot, tucked in between these two grungy motorhomes. That's when I spot Skip and Gill taking a break over by their trailer. I didn't think anything of it at first. Gill brought over a couple plates of food, dropped one in front of Skip, and the other for himself. As I'm watching I notice something odd; Skip's food is moving.

I almost dropped my bag of weed when I saw that. Focusing on his food I can see that it looks like spaghetti, but wriggles like worms. I mean, I knew carnies were strange, but to eat a plate full of raw worms was pretty gross. Looking at Gilligan's plate I didn't even know what he was eating. Honestly it looked like someone had taken a crap on his plate.

Maybe it was some kind of bratwurst…*right?*

I had just lit the joint and taken a hit when Skip reached up and pulled off his face. That's right; *I said he pulled off his face.* I swear; I almost crapped a cinder block when I saw that. Where his face should have been was now a pair of these big, buggy eyes and a mouth surrounded by a dozen or so tentacles. He leans over the plate and the tentacles start pulling worms into his mouth. The whole time he's making this slurping sound like he's eating spaghetti.

I was just thinking that the weed was making me hallucinate when Gill pulls off his own face. He's got big bug eyes too, but instead of a mouth he has this… snout. That's the best word I can think of. Anyhow, Gill spits this gob of goo on his plate, and the food… or whatever it was… starts hissing and dissolving. Next thing, he stoops over the plate and uses that snout to slurp up the brown mess.

By this time, I'd completely forgotten about the joint in my hand. My jaw was hanging open, and I was trying to think of what to do when I realize that I'm not alone. I look behind me and there stands Lurch from the spook-house. That time I think I really did crap my pants, or at least I sharted a little into my tightey-whiteys. I wanted to run away but my feet wouldn't oblige. Staring down at me like Frankenstein's monster, Lurch's eyes looked even more dead than usual. I was sure he was going to snap my neck like a chicken, or suck my soul out of my body. But instead he just said one word.

"Move." The creepy giant grumbled, shoving me

in the back.

As soon as I stepped out of the shadows, Skip and Gill both stood up in surprise. Reattaching their faces in a big hurry, Gill didn't get his on quite right. With half his face drooping he looked at me with those doll-eyes.

Lurch nudged me along until I was standing in front of the two. The whole time I kept wondering if they would melt me with their death ray or replace me with a mask-wearing copy. I'd seen movies like *The Blob*, *Invasion of the Body Snatchers*, and *War of the Worlds*, so I was pretty well convinced that these guys weren't here for the betterment of mankind. Maybe to *serve* mankind… on a dinner platter!

"You… you aren't gonna eat me are you?" I managed to get the words out as my teeth chattered in fear.

Skipper and Gilligan made a series of clicking noises as they looked back and forth between one another. It took me a moment to realize that they were laughing. Worse yet, they were not laughing <u>with</u> me.

"Eat a *hey-uman*!" Gill seemed to find the idea preposterous.

"Ewww." Skip paused long enough to show open revulsion. "Most of you don't even bathe."

I was shocked by that, but still; I was sure they were up to no good.

"Then you're gonna attach a parasite to my back and use it to control me… like they did in *Puppet Masters*!" I'd just finished reading Robert Heinlein's novel the week before so I was sure I had a lock on what was about to happen.

"Stupid *hoo-mans*." Shaking his head, Lurch walked past me before jabbing a finger at Gill. "He's your problem. I gots 'ta eat."

Although I was still terrified about what was about to happen, I was pretty surprised at the casual disregard that the big guy had just shown. It was like he didn't care that I'd just found them out.

"No, we're not going to attach a parasite." Shaking his head, Skip's mask flopped about on one side where it had not been properly fastened.

"Then you're here to take over humanity, aren't you?" I was sure that I'd figured out their master plan.

"Kid," Skip started out. "If you had the chance, would you go down to the Amazon and use your technology to take over a tribe of cannibals?"

I gave that some thought before answering. "What in the hell for?"

"Zactly!" Skip pointed a finger at me in agreement.

I was sure that they were here to turn humanity into a buffet line when I noticed Lurch sit down at the table with a basket of broccoli. Pulling off his mask revealed a face that was almost entirely mouth, with a single eye on a short little stalk. Paying no attention to me, he began shoving the green plants into his maw. I remember being surprised that the scariest of them all was a vegetarian. *Really?*

"Then what are you doing here on Earth? Or if you tell me will you have to wipe my memories?"

Something was not adding up here. Feeling a dose of confidence, I decided not to run away... *yet.*

"Wipe his mind..." Gill E. Gann made the chattering sound again.

"Naw kid, we don't gotta wipe your mind. It's not like anyone is going to believe you." Seemingly confident, Skipper took a moment to reattach his mask properly.

"We're here to study *hey-umans.*" Gill answered the other half of my question.

"No way!" I rejected that right away. "You set up a whole carnival just so you can scare people in the spook house?"

Gill made a strange face as part of his mask hung askew. "It only looks like an ordinary carnival. The spook house is actually a neural scanner. We give you a good scare, then measure the reaction of your central nervous system. Mister Urch over there is writing his thesis on the cognitive abilities of evolving species."

"Evolving species?" I was stung by the insult.

"Seriously kid," Skip clucked at me. "Your people still practice organized tactical extermination."

I was having a hard time figuring out what he was talking about when Gill filled in the blanks.

"I think they call it... war."

Nodding in agreement, Skip snapped his fingers. "Yeah, you *hey-umans* still practice war. It's a good thing you haven't managed to escape from this solar system yet."

I had to agree with him on that one. We humans were definitely a violent bunch of sociopaths. Even more incredible; people like me who advocated for peace were called hippies and other derogatory terms. *How crazy is that, right?*

"Oh yeah, well then what's the Gravitron for?" I pointed to the big spinning ride that pinned riders to the walls.

"Oooh, that's an excellent place to study *hey-uman* muscle and bone density under increased gravitational loading." Giving an awkward smile, it was clear that Gill was still getting the hang of facial expressions. "Skip and I are studying alien physiology for our graduate studies."

Something seemed to click in my head.

"Wait a minute, you're all post-graduate students... same as me?" Suddenly they didn't seem so alien after all.

Nodding in unison, Skip and Gill confirmed my statement. Behind them I could see big Lurch shoving a whole ear of corn into that gaping hole in his face.

"Well, all of us except Miss Endora." Gill reminded his compatriot before turning back to me. "She's our professor on this expedition."

I thought of the woman with the sharp eyes that inhabited the main ticket booth. It occurred to me that I'd never seen her outside of the booth. Did she even have legs?

"So, you guys all chose names from TV shows to what... blend in?" I had started to see a pattern. Everyone knew about Endora from Bewitched, and Gilligan's Island was on prime-time TV every week. Not only that, but shows like the Munsters and the

Addams Family had been around for years. Back then there were only three networks so we all pretty much watched the same shows and movies.

"Seemed like a good idea, and no one pays any attention to the carnies." Skip folded his arms as if he was proud of their subterfuge.

Although everything they said seemed plausible, I was still not sold.

"What about the tunnel of love? What're ya studying there?"

"*Hey-uman* mating rituals." Skipper answered without hesitation. "Gomez and Morticia are co-authoring their dissertation on *hey-uman* conjugal interactions."

"What about the merry-go-round?" I asked, giving them a hard look. I wanted to know everything.

"Oh, that." Gill chuckled. "That we added just because it's... relaxing. Sometimes after the place closes for the night we fire it up and ride it just for fun."

"I like to ride 'da horsies." From his spot at the table, big ol' Lurch nodded enthusiastically.

"Look kid, we'd love to talk all night with you, but our dinner break is running out." Ever the serious one, Skipper gestured to the half-eaten plate of worms that still squirmed on the table. It looked like a few of the things were trying to escape from the dish.

"So that's it?" I was surprised. "You're not gonna wipe my memory?"

"Like I said, no one is going to believe you."

Turning away, Skip began to seat his portly frame at the wooden park table.

"But I have so many questions." I didn't mean to, but my voice had a bit of a whine to it.

Pulling off his face again, Gill used his proboscis to slurp up the rest of the goo on his plate. Sitting down at the table beside him I couldn't help but notice the stench of his dinner.

"What is that stuff anyhow? It smells like shit." Making a distasteful face I pointed at the remaining brown sausage on his plate.

"*Hey-uman* fecal matter." Answering in a cheery voice, Gill wiped his snout with a dirty sleeve.

That's when I realized that it was exactly what I had first thought it was. "You mean that's a human turd?"

"It's quite a delicacy on my planet. They're marvelous when you freeze them solid, with just a dash of cyanide." The lips on the end of his snout seemed to quiver at the thought. I tried to imagine him enjoying a tasty turd-popsicle.

"Look kid," Skip turned to me as the tentacles on his face gripped a dozen squirming worms. "I'll make you a deal. You can ask us questions, but we get to ask you stuff too."

"Really?" I was surprised that it would be so easy.

"Sure." Gill nodded eagerly, his bug eyes aglow. "There are many things about your species that are very... nuanced. Like for instance, why do you suck on that burning stick?"

I'd been so surprised by the whole turn of events that I had forgotten I still had the joint in my hand.

Although it had long since gone out, I'd been clutching it the whole time.

"Oh that; it's marijuana. It gets me stoned." I gave a broad smile as I held the doober up for them to examine.

"You mean it calcifies you?" Skip did not seem to get the reference.

"Oh, no, no. I mean it makes me feel mellow. Y'know, it enhances the world, makes me feel happy." I looked back and forth between those alien faces hoping that they'd understand. "It makes food taste better, music sound better."

They seemed to consider this for a moment before Lurch spoke up in that deep baritone voice of his.

"Could I scan you while you... smoke it?" Reattaching his face, he seemed truly curious.

The thought pleased me. "You mean I'd be getting stoned for science? Hells yeah!"

The job lasted for another two weeks before they packed up shop and moved on to another planet somewhere in the Proxima-Centauri system. But during those days we exchanged a ton of knowledge. It had been fascinating as I came to see them not as an invasive alien species, but rather as college students not much different from me.

That was almost fifty years ago. Since then I have managed to rack up ten Hugo awards in science fiction, and more than a dozen Nebulas. Whenever my fans ask me where I get my ideas from, I just smile and tell them they'd never believe me if I told them. But to this day I like to look up at the stars and think about the friends I made back in the summer of '66. I can't help but wonder if they ever look up at their own stars and think of me.

To find more about Ralph Rotten and his books,
visit
www.indiesunited.net/ralph-rotten

SUSPENSE

The Taxi Driver

Timothy R. Baldwin

Drops of rain fell on a faded gray sedan, labeled *Charlie's Cab Company*, which sat in an otherwise bare parking lot. Charlie, the owner, stood next to the car. In his hands he clasped an envelope he didn't dare to open for fear of forewarned repercussion. Rain fell on Charlie until tiny creeks flowed between the wrinkles around his eyes and trickled down his cheeks. An endless sea of gray clouds told him that driving today would be dreadful, but he had to do it…

Last night's final fare occurred because of a choice Charlie made. This choice proved to be dangerous, but not because of his passengers; a young couple recently married.

When the young husband gave out directions, Charlie cringed. He knew the route through the mountains would be treacherous. A passing thought urged him to leave the young couple at the restaurant on Main Street. In his moment of hesitation, he recalled tales told in his childhood of married couples on dark, winding roads.

Charlie shook the thought away and smiled at the husband and wife, both of whom teetered on the curb, drunk. Charlie invited them into the cab. The husband helped his giggling wife into her seat before he stumbled his way around the car and got in the back. The wife snuggled next to her husband, closed her eyes, and sighed.

The couple was clearly in love, and Charlie, though distant was his memory of young love, could still relate.

He drove through the fog as Phil—the name he overheard the wife call her husband—gave directions over his wife's drunken giggles and slurred speech. Her name, Charlie would later discover, was Alice. As Charlie drove, Phil and Alice sat in the back seat and spoke in whispers occasionally broken by a joke or some story only understood by those riding the buzz of a late-night party. Charlie was glad that Phil was sober enough to guide him around one dark, foggy bend in the back road, then another.

Though short in miles, the trip seemed like an eternity, primarily because Charlie fought the weight of sleepiness. Eventually, he lost the battle, as his head bobbed and his eyes closed. Somewhere between awake and dreaming, he swerved to the left, then to the right, until a horn from an oncoming truck blared.

"You okay, pal?" Phil asked.

Charlie nodded, pinched the bridge of his nose and continued driving.

The winding back roads eventually led to a brightly-lit mansion on a hill. As Phil and his wife got out and paid their fare, Phil placed his hands on the car door, leaned in the open window and whispered, "Say, buddy... it's late."

Phil paused and looked over his shoulder. His wife stumbled over one of the steps leading up to the mansion.

"I'm okay," Alice said with a giggle. "Just need to rest for a moment."

Phil turned back to Charlie. "We thought you might want to come in and sleep in our guest bedroom."

Charlie looked at his watch— 4:05 am. In all his years as a cab driver, no one had ever invited him in. Odd as the invitation was, he was tired, and agreed to stay the night.

"Great," Phil smiled. "Can you help me with my wife? Alice had a little too much to drink."

After locking the door and grabbing from the trunk a small duffle bag which he kept packed for emergencies, Charlie hoisted Alice from one side while her husband did the same on the other. Together, the two men carried a nearly unconscious young bride into the house. After three flights of steps, they laid her in bed and turned off the lights. The two men then headed down four flights of steps, the fourth of which led to a basement, where they stood in a sparsely, though comfortably furnished little bedroom.

"I'd offer you a nightcap..." Phil began.

"That's okay," Charlie said. "It's late... or should I

say early."

Phil nodded without emotion. "Maybe both."

"I appreciate the accommodations," Charlie said. "I'm pretty sure I wouldn't make it back home otherwise."

"You take care," Phil said and clapped Charlie on the shoulders. "We'll see you off in the morning."

After Phil left the room, Charlie locked the door, shut off the lights, and collapsed on the bed. Sleep overtook his tired body until a bang and the splintering of wood caused him to stir. A blinding light illuminated the hallway and seared through Charlie's closed eyelids. He groaned and attempted to roll over, but found himself unable to do so. Opening his eyes, he squinted. A flashlight shone in his face. Charlie could barely make out the movement of a person just beyond the light.

"Charlie," a distorted voice spoke. "You've been selected."

"Phil? Alice?" Charlie couldn't tell whether the voice came from a man or a woman.

"Neither."

Charlie said, "Then where am—?"

"Oh, you're still where you've always been," the voice continued. "Only you've forced us to change the game."

Charlie cleared his throat. He thought back to his most recent fare. It couldn't have been any more than a few hours ago. The only thing he had done differently was to accept the hospitality of two strangers for the night.

"Oh, no." The voice seemed to chuckle as if

reading Charlie's thoughts. "It wasn't anything you did last night or even the night before. It was time."

From somewhere in the darkness, another set of footsteps approached. Charlie heard the ripping of duct tape. He squirmed, but as he did, he found himself held fast by several hands. One set held his wrists, while another set removed blankets, then his t-shirt. A cold metal object placed on his chest caused Charlie to pull away, but hands held him fast. With deliberate care, another set of hands secured the metal object to his chest with one layer after another layer of tape. As he was being tied down, the thought running through Charlie's mind was singular—*I hope I'm around to feel the pain of removing that tape later.*

After his head and arms were shoved back into his t-shirt, Charlie was hoisted to his feet, blindfolded, and pushed up the stairs and through a door.

Though blindfolded, Charlie sensed he was now outside. His captors allowed a brief pause as Charlie pointed his eyes toward the sky. Sunlight penetrated through the fabric of the blindfold, yet he was unable to sense the exact time of day. A heavy hand prodded him forward.

His feet shuffled on concrete, then blacktop, as his captors led him down a set of steps. Somehow, he knew he was still at the mansion.

Breathing a little easier because he had gained his bearings, Charlie was not at all surprised to hear the latch of the driver's side door of his taxi-cab click open. He was shoved toward the open door and told to sit. He reached for his blindfold.

"Not yet," the distorted voice from before whispered in his ear. "Open your hand."

Charlie complied. A moment later, he held a small square object.

"Do not remove the blindfold until you hear this phone ring," the voice said. "When it rings, answer it."

The door slammed. Moments passed in silence as Charlie listened.

The phone rang. Charlie tore the blindfold from his eyes and tossed it into the back seat. As the phone rang again, he lifted his t-shirt. A black object secured tightly to his chest by duct tape flashed a series of numbers on a small LCD console. Time ticking.

The phone rang again. Charlie was sure it had rung several times, so he answered it and hoped he had not pissed off the person on the other end.

An undistorted woman's voice on the other end of the phone spoke first. "Say a word to the police, and you die," she said. "Do you understand?"

"But—"

"Why?" she interrupted. "Simple. You asked for it."

"I don't—"

"Do you understand our demands so far?"

"Yes."

"Good."

Silence.

He lifted his shirt once again. A small red light next to the LCD screen of the box attached to his chest blinked twice.

"No need to check," the woman's voice continued.

"We're monitoring your every move. You have forty-five minutes to meet our demands. Reach beneath your seat and open the envelope."

Charlie did as he was told and found a white printout paper and another, smaller, envelope that read, *For Anna's eyes only*. He unfolded the printout:

1. Consequences for Anna's envelope will be unfortunate.
2. Keep the phone on you at all times.
3. Go to First National Bank on Main Street.
4. Hand the teller, Anna, her envelope.

You now have 44 minutes. Destroy this note and be on your way.

Charlie glanced at the box beneath his shirt. Sure enough, forty-five minutes remained. He glanced in his rearview mirror, then up toward the mansion. It seemed eerily abandoned. The driveway was empty, and the porch lights were off. No one was in sight.

Perhaps, Charlie thought, the car Phil and Alice took to the party still sat in a parking garage on Main Street.

"Charlie," the woman's voice on the phone screamed. "Get moving."

He set the phone down, buckled his seatbelt, and turned the key. The taxi's engine hesitated and conked out. He swore and turned the key again. He pushed on the gas pedal and the engine roared. The car squealed as Charlie sped out of the driveway.

Back on the winding road, which he had been down the night before, Charlie realized the note, now crumpled and damp with sweat, was still clenched in his hand.

Destroy this note.

He crumpled it in a ball, stuffed it in his mouth, and slowly chewed the paper as he rounded another bend in the road.

Arriving in town, Charlie turned down Main Street, a two-lane, one-way road which led north toward several farms owned mostly by Amish families. The next turn he made brought him into the parking lot of the First National Bank. Circling the small parking lot so that his car faced the exit, he pulled in and cranked the parking brake.

A quick lift of his shirt showed ten minutes remained on the LCD screen. His watch showed 9:55 am. He had five minutes before the bank opened. He looked up, and large drops of rain began to land on his windshield.

"Great," he muttered. He got out of the car, grabbed the envelope, shoved it beneath his shirt, and closed the door.

For a few moments, Charlie stood in the rain until it trickled down his cheeks. He checked his watch, then looked up at the bank. He pulled out the envelope and held it tightly.

"Pleasure. Adventure. Is there a difference?" He smiled, then wiped the tiny creeks of rain from around his eyes. He headed toward the bank and a blonde-haired woman unlocked the front door and held it open for him as he entered.

"Welcome to First National," she said with a smile. "What can we do for you?"

Charlie glanced at her name tag, which read, *Anna*. He handed her the envelope.

As Anna opened the envelope, her smile faded. She locked the bank door, then signaled another woman who sat behind a desk in a windowed office. Charlie turned in her direction and raised his shirt revealing the counter.

00:15:29

The second woman surreptitiously hit a button beneath her desk, then stood and smiled.

The telephone in Charlie's hand rang. He answered it.

"Well done, Charlie," the woman's voice spoke.

"What do you—" Charlie heard a click. "Hello!" he yelled.

The deathly silence at the other end gave him the dreaded answer.

Sirens blaring in the distance grew louder as police cars approached the bank. Uniformed officers and a swat team surrounded the bank.

Charlie was alone with no recourse upon which to fall. No proof of his coercion.

Later, the local newspaper published Charlie's story on the fifth page of the first section of the Sunday paper with the following headline and corresponding story:

CAB DRIVER HOLDS UP BANK
WITH FALSE BOMB

Claims he "was forced"

A 57-year-old man was arrested on Tuesday morning as he attempted to rob the First National Bank with a fake bomb strapped to his chest. The retired steelworker turned independent taxi driver maintained that he had been abducted early Tuesday morning from the home of his last fare. Upon further investigation, police detectives determined that the man had stayed in the basement of a condemned mansion located in the mountains just south of town. Detectives found DNA and forensic evidence which indicated that the 57-year-old man had been living in the basement of the home for several years. At this time, they have made no connections between the man's most recent activities and the thirty-year-old mansion fire. The mansion, once owned by Phil and Alice Johnson, was condemned. No one knows what happened to the Johnsons.

To find out more about Timothy R. Baldwin and his books, visit
www.indiesunited.net/timothy-baldwin

Fall

PARANORMAL

A Necromancer and the Cheshire Cat

S.R. Ruark

Tass leaned against the private plane's window as they circled the next property to be viewed. The window was warm against her skin from the bright sun. No clouds blocked the heat, even the knife-thin facial scars felt warm for once. Looking down, Tass saw old-growth forest mixed alongside flatland plains. Areas where scrub was trying to reclaim former farmland. The sun not quite at zenith making the world look almost new still. Scar tissue along her left cheek were cool lines, contrasting with the warm skin.

"Ms. Cathead, we're approaching the old Wale property. Would you like to…" The realtor tried to engage her reclusive client, admiring the white silk sleeveless blouse the girl was wearing. The arms were muscular if thin, and more than slightly scared.

"Stop," Tass said quietly. She turned to look at the older woman across from her. The girl's gold and amethyst chandelier earrings emphasized her eyes, amber-gold with a scattering of dark purple in the iris, the warmth from the earrings more palatable than the warmth in the girl's eyes.

Mrs. Verigon, stopped mid thought on her spiel, to look through her property listings. The young lady's list of necessities had been short but what she wanted was very specific. Good farm land with a graveyard on the land, the older the graveyard the better, and far enough from the main four cities to be considered on the outskirts of civilization. Mrs. Verigon wasn't sure if Ms. Cathead just wanted a challenge of farming or, if rumors were anything to go by, away from grasping parents she was recently emancipated from. Either way, the farmlands listed were not exactly easy to come by.

Tass sat up as she focused on a dilapidated three story white and grey house. "Is this where we are landing?"

"What dear?"

"That house." She pointed to a rapidly approaching ground structure.

"No... we are going to the Wales house three miles due north."

"Down."

"What?"

"Go down here." Tass stabbing a finger at the glass, pointing emphatically. "I want to look at this house. Land here." Her voice brooked no argument. The older woman blinked at the commanding tone, but Mrs. Verigon merely nodded. One did indulge the clients, even the...odd ones. She stood up in the small plane, smoothing her dark red skirt, an unconscious motion on her way to the cockpit.

Tass looked down at the sprawling house. She could almost hear something even this far up and she wanted to listen to those voices.

The plan started to tilt slowly, lowering their altitude.

"The captain said it would be a few moments as he needs to find a flattish area to land," Mrs. Verigon chirped as she walked back towards Tass.

Tass gave a sharp nod to Mrs. Verigon, concentrating on the rising landscape, dismissing the realtor. The realtor bit her lip on the child's rudeness but reminded herself that Dancers, especially the very successful and rich Dancers were an odd and dangerous lot.

"Is there something about this area that you feel is special, dear?" Mrs. Verigon asked hesitantly, her hand was outstretched; however, Mrs. Verigon knew better than to touch an ex-Dancer without her permission.

"I can hear the dead," Tass said cocking her head. "They almost sound happy."

Mrs. Verigon sat up a little straighter. "Are any still moving?"

Tass had to concentrate only for a moment. "No. They have all been laid to rest but more than a few have not moved on. I am curious as to why." The girl went back to staring out the window, with narrowed eyes, her nose almost pressing against the glass as if that would hurry the plane's landing.

Mrs. Verigon swallowed hard, but tried for a perky voice. "Well then, we shall see what is down there." She had never liked zombies, even as a small child; ghosts were more acceptable. Something that would not make her want to run screaming back to the cities as fast as the plane could carry her.

The hover plane landed to the right of the house, with only a few bumps. Mrs. Verigon clutched the leather seat arm rests tightly during the turbulence. Tass could barely contain her impatience as the pilot let down the stairs.

Tass unsnapped her seatbelt as soon as the plane stopped, heading for the door. The latch was simple to open now that the plane had landed. A quick twist and Tass was able to hop down the stairs to the house at a quick walk. She didn't wait for the bodyguard Mrs. Verigon had brought along for the rough viewing areas.

The bodyguard was quick to follow without an invitation from the blond girl. The dark-skinned man, with blue highlights in his long braid, tucked into a bun, with smaller braids along the sides, was out the plane following on Tass' heels. His eyes always moving and one hand on his disc pistol. The bodyguard's scrolling arm tattoo in silver and gold shimmered in the sun, subtle against dark skin.

Tass stopped in front of the house, her head bowed and slightly tilted to the left. Mrs. Verigon went to talk to her but was stopped by a well-muscled arm of the bodyguard.

"Why are you stopping me?" she snapped, not seeing any dangers for the bodyguard to be touching her for.

"Not while she's talking to the dead, unless you

want to lose a chunk of flesh to one of her zombies?"

"She can't raise a zombie out here! No bodies under 100 years may be raised."

"This land has a fuck-ton more than 100-year-old zombies." The man said with the disdain used to talk to a very slow adult with little common sense.

"And this should worry me how?" Mrs. Verigon asked with narrowed eyes, her shoulders tight, anger lacing her voice as she slammed her left fist onto a hip.

"She could pull zombies enough up to bury you, me, and that plane, and never break a sweat. If, and that if is always contingent on how sane the necromancer is, she wanted to." The man gave a slight smile, showing only the bottom edges of his teeth.

"How would you..." she asked with a sneer, insinuating that a 3rd rate bodyguard would understand anything, "know what she can or cannot do?"

"I studied her and her sisters' old fights," the bodyguard said, lowering his arm from the realtor's shoulders. "Those two could pull the dead faster and from further than either let on." Again with that slight smile. "I am betting there are more than a few extra bodies tucked here and there due to those two than the Arena can account for." The bodyguard looked at the almost innocent looking slim-hipped girl in grey slacks with the admiration of one athlete for another.

Mrs. Verigon swallowed once more. "I'll get some water for us, shall I?" and she beat a well-manicured retreat on 3-inch heels. She made it to the hover plane with only a minor wobble or two in the tall grass.

"Was scaring her really necessary?" Tass asked the bodyguard after as Mrs. Verigon left.

"Yes." The man grinned. "She has no clue what it takes to raise or fight the dead." With a slight shrug, "Plus it adds to your mystique."

Tass tossed a glare over her shoulder, causing the man to flash his broken-tooth smile wider.

"I should have the undead grab your feet," she muttered but she didn't really mean it. Much.

"There are that many undead here you could do that?"

It was Tass' turn to flash an evil smile with very white regular teeth. She knew how to rattle a fighting Dancer.

"Fuck, if I had known that I'd have asked for double the pay." The man crossed his hands over his wiry chest, but he did keep a closer eye on the ground they tread. "Necromancers are all crazy," he muttered aloud.

"I heard that!"

"Woulda been wasted if you hadn't," the dark-skinned man said with a toss of his head, loose smaller braids clacking together softly as he laughed.

The realtor came back with a few pouches of water. The guard was watching the girl as she seemed to be listening to the ground and the house. She would stare for a moment then wander off. The guard kept his eyes on her and the surrounding shoulder high grass and brush. This area could hide more than a few things that would leave a nasty scar.

"What is she doing?" the realtor hissed.

"Probably talking to the dead still," the bodyguard said just as softly.

"Are they really that loud?"

"Louder for the necromancers than it ever will be for you or I."

"How the hell can that be? We're living," she snapped, unconsciously outraged that a dead body could be better company than her well-heeled self could be.

He gave her a quick, disgusted look. "You're not trying to get her attention. You want her to buy the land while you get your commission and go away." Disdainfully, he added, "The dead are dead. No one listens to them. Except necromancers. And the dead know this. The stronger the Power, the easier they hear every undead whisper, cry, or scream. The living cannot compete... except for a mother's newborn child. Maybe. If the babe is lucky." His eyes kept looking left and right, head turned slightly but eyes always moving.

Tass walked around the house with its peeling paint of white and grey and almost cheerful dark blue shutters. She stopped at several patches of mostly overgrown grass patches marked in rusting thigh-high ornate wrought wire. She nodded her head to a conversation that the other two could not hear.

The guard stiffened when Tass's head turned to the left sharply looking to the head-high grass. She was nodding to an unheard conversation. The grass bent against the push of the wind. The bodyguards hand unlocked his disc gun, easing it out.

"Don't," Tass said.

"Dangerous?"

"Not to us." She stopped to listen. "The Cheshire isn't hungry or desperate enough to attack all of us."

"There's more than just one of those out here."

"The frogs are another issue, and not close today, I'm told." With a shrug Tass headed back to the plane. "I'll take it," she commented to the realtor, plucking a globe of water from the realtor's un-responsive hand. The conversation between the Dancer and the guard going over her head.

"I... not on the list. I'll need to find out who to..." she stuttered.

"Davin," Tass responded, her eyes moving over the yard and house again with a faint smile playing over her lips as she took a pull of the drink.

"Excuse me?" The realtor's voice was incredulous.

"Davin is the sole survivor and he lives in one of the cities." Tass took a sip. "Madile wasn't sure which city but he is the only one left in the family."

"Madile?"

"The original owner. She passed the land to her middle son, Morganus." Tass looked around the yard not really seeing the here and now. "He was the only one who wanted to farm. The rest up and moved."

"Leaving Davin as the final living relative?"

"Yes!" Tass looked both pleased and relieved that the realtor finally followed her train of thought. With a last nod she headed into the hover plane.

"I'll get on that right now." The realtor pulled out

her laptop, tapping her neck collar.

"Dysic, I need to look for a Davin who is the owner of land in the wilds." She started tapping one manicured blue nail on her pad. "If I knew the last name, I wouldn't need to send you the coordinates or even call you, now would I?" Her sarcasm was acidic to her office underling. So engrossed was she that she didn't even mind the bodyguard's hand on the small of her back helping to herd her into the plane. Tass had moved into the plane, ready to return to the city and start talking to her lawyer about the land purchase.

Tass sat looking out the window, ignoring the talking realtor and the quiet guard. She wore a small musing smile as the plane took off.

The striped iridescent purple and light blue Cheshire stepped from the grass, with horizontal slit eyes narrowed to a hair-thin line as it watched the strange machine rise up into the bright blue sky. The mouth opened almost to the large furry ears, exposing sharp pointed teeth in a yawn. The Cheshire stretched then went to her favorite place in the tree next to the white not-tree. The branch was 10 feet from the ground and curving just so horizontally, a good fit the long, lean felinoid body. Her tail dangled only a couple feet from the ground. She could watch for unwary prey to wander into the yard from her vantage. She felt mild concern for the unusual bird that had come into her Territory but the small furry food that the bird had frightened into her waiting paws made up for her concern with a full stomach.

"Tass." Jerico was only slightly irritated. When he was really irritated, he used her first and last name. "This is a huge purchase and the renovations will take at least half of your bank account."

"But just the one account. Yes?" She leaned against the grey silk couch, staring out of the window, watching the clouds roll in, hiding the city's skyscrapers. The silk matched the plush throw rugs over white flagstone flooring.

"Yes." A heavy sigh. "Just the main one." Jerico tried for professional calm.

"I can hear your disapproval," Tass said with a smile, amused, as her hand restlessly twitched, fiddling with the blue tassels on the gold and blue pillow. Several other throw pillows of bright colors were scattered like careless gems around the couch and floor, breaking the monotony of grey and white.

"Your parents will file suit to stop you from 'squandering' your money." Anger threaded through his professional voice. Very few people saw through her parents' caring adoring public façade; Jerico was one of a handful.

Tass could imagine him, in his office with tightened jaw clamping down on white teeth, not saying what was really going through his mind.

"They sued last time and got their bank account drained far more than they wanted after the last purchase they tried to fight," she said egging him on, but only slightly. He had had enough run-ins with them in and out of court to despise them as much as she and Torri.

"They may have better legal grounds this time." His voice dropped in tone with worry.

"I'm emancipated, yes?"

"By the skin of your teeth. If they can prove you are doing too many narcotics or show a habit of recklessness, they could try to have you committed."

"Luckily I have you to block them from their own stupidity."

Jerico was silent for a moment. "Tass, we've covered this before, however…"

"No." Tass sat up with a snarl, her fist balling at her side. A small alarm went off on the side wall, by the front door, next to the aquarium filled halfway with dirt. The dirt was starting to move.

"I can hear the alarm going." Jerico said gently as he tried for calm.

Tass took three deep breaths, pushing out the irritation. The alarm subsided as the dirt stopped moving.

"Better." Tass clenched her jaw this time. "And the answer is still no. I will NOT pay my parents an allowance to keep them away from me." Tass' lips lifted in a silent snarl; the alarm blinked a warning as a tremor was detected in the dirt but not movement.

"Doroigan-"

"Is crippled and subsisting on his former glory after they drained him dry." Tass pinched the bridge of her nose in anger. She shook her head to look at the tranquil skyline again, searching for elusive calm. "He won't be able to maintain the stipends he uses, but he will continue long past the point of driving him onto the streets just to keep them away."

"Your sister pays them," Jerico said, pushing back against her stubbornness. The same stubbornness that had kept both sisters alive during the Dances.

"But only from out of her caretaker's paycheck. NOT from her Dancing accounts," Tass said with a sniff at her sister's unwillingness to fight.

"Thankfully your parents don't know that." Jerico breathed a sigh of relief.

"Be thankful they haven't figured out a legal way to come after you since you're sleeping with her. Or how much she really makes at the hospital," Tass said with edged humor, looking at the phone with both exasperation and fondness.

"Ugh. Now you're being bitchy." But she could hear his laughter that took the sting out of the comment.

"Then stop bringing up my parents," she said in aggrieved tones, her fists clenching and unclenching.

"My job as your lawyer to cover all the issues, not just the purchasing." Jerico waited for a moment for Tass' response. When none were forthcoming, he cleared his throat to bring her back to the here and now. "Tass."

"I hear you." Tass stared back out the window. The view was magnificent at 40 floors up. "If it makes you feel better and if you think it will keep them off your ass for allowing this, emphasize how dangerous the outliers' areas are. If I die, they are likely to inherit." This time her eyes narrowed as she growled out the comment.

"That area isn't very dangerous. Only yellow/green." Jerico wasn't buying her spin on the property to protect her from the impending parental lawsuit.

"But red for Necromancers," she said smugly.

Jerico sucked in his breath. "They will protest over this." His voice dropping to a whisper. Yellow was well within her ability but red was nothing to trifle with when dealing with PTSD as well.

"This is why you emphasis the inheritance if I die," she snapped tartly back.

"Your will doesn't leave them more than the cost for a box seat at the Stadium. And that is for one, not two, I might add," he said, slightly snippy in return. He would be dealing with the fallout and lawsuits from her parents, not her, if she died.

"Yeah," a cold smile flitted across her face. She had paid for that will with blood and more money than she had wanted, but it would be worth every penny not going to her parents for an iron-clad protected last will and testament. "I know. But they don't."

"Evil and exactingly cruel," Jerico's voice held approval.

"Now will you write your proposal and see if we can't get a better price than the one offered by Ms. Verigan?" She was almost petulant. Almost.

"Do you plan to sell your penthouse?"

Tass had to stop and think. This idea new to her. "Hmm...hadn't considered it. It was a gift." The elderly couple who had gifted it to her did so after they had made a killing betting on her and her sister during the third worst Dance in the twins' career. Tass still had nightmares of the sand ants and warriors with nets.

"A very nice gift that you won't need when you move," Jerico pointed out. "And I won't even suggest letting your parents have it. Though that would sweeten their greed for a month or two?"

She ignored the comment of her parents. "Where would I stay? The hotels are nice but they don't have rising alarms," she mused.

"We have 3 alarms. We can acquire a 4th if you need a place to stay when you visit."

Tass grinned. "Really? I know how much you hate the alarms."

"Dead things in glass aquariums are not my idea of house decoration." The sigh was heavy. He had lost the argument when faced with the facts of how likely a powerful necro was to raise anything or everything dead within range; human or animal and some things should never be raised on a colonized world. He had given in, but had insisted that the warning riser cabinets have wood finish with metal etched screens that looked a part of the decorations besides bare glass with dirt.

"Necessary though."

"For you and your sister, absolutely." Jerico hesitated. "If you are truly set on this, I will help. Promise me, you'll be careful out there yes?

"I promise." This time Tass' voice grew hoarse. "I can't stand staying this close to my parents. I need to leave. What they did to Titon and Dorigan..." Tass blinked rapidly, trying to stall the tears; she couldn't finish the sentence even as one tear slid down her face. She wiped it away angrily with a shake of her head.

"Yes, Tass. I will take care of it." Jerico's voice was gentle. He had held Torri through many nightmares concerning her parents and a few from the Dances.

"Thank you. Give Torri a hug for me when you see her." Tass' voice was less gravely but the pain was still there. Jerico could hear it.

"That will be tonight, and I will be very happy to give her your hug." Jerico said with a smile as he hung up the phone.

Tass stood with a slow stretch up then put her hands to the floor feeling the pull of muscles and scar tissue. She stood up, walking to the aquarium, to smooth the dirt back over her alarm.

Three weeks later, Jerico had come through for her. He had negotiated a far better term for the land then Tass had any right to expect. Half the estimated land value in cash with an exchange for box seat season tickets for the next five years of any Dance at any arena of the seller's choice, for two. Davin had jumped on that deal faster than the real-estate agent could say yeah or nay. Her cut was somewhat reduced, but Jerico sweetened her deal with another pair of Season tickets for two years. She would make a killing selling the tickets or make connections if she decided to attend. She also very happy with the land sale even if the sale had not been completely what she had originally bargained for.

Any retired Dancer was entitled to six tickets to any Dance, in or out of Season game, at any of the three Arenas. Tass never used hers, allowing Jerico to sell them for extra money into her retirement account. Seven seasons of Dancing, with the last three in the top 10 spot for necromancers, had given Tass enough time on the sands that she would never willingly step back in any Arena. Her parents were not allowed to use any of her tickets or the sales of; they were barred from attempting to use her name to gain access to the reserved box seats. All arenas had this noted in their systems on the understanding that Jerico's firm would sue them for a multitude of violations. That was but one of the many court battles Tass had had to fight to keep her parents from profiting off of her as a former Dancer.

The judge had pointed out that as former Dancers themselves, they already had more tickets than they were using as none of their children would willingly sit with them at any Dance. Her parents' greed was becoming well known by that point, earning scorn in many vectors.

"Are you sure?" Was all Torri asked, when Jerico presented the key to Tass over dinner at the new posh Katherian restaurant.

Two seasons out of the Dance and the twins still turned heads as they walked into the restaurant. Torri and Tass had once again mimicked each other unknowingly, for dinner. Each wore an ankle length dress draped over one shoulder, split up the hip, showing well-muscled if scared thighs. Torri went with her customary dark red while Tass wore a deep almost violet sapphire blue. Their hair was fashionably loose, instead of their Dancer braided upswept hair.

Jerico escorted both to their low table, with a reed mat for each to sit on, redolent of freshly cut grass and brilliant brocaded lounging pillows. The pillows were large enough for either a Wolfen or Katherian, and could have made a bed for either woman. Jerico and Torri shared a seat, showing open affection, with frequent kisses and hand holding, to the dismay of the older patrons.

Tass grinned at the eddies of disruption the three of them made. The wait staff handled the unexpected arrival of the twins with aplomb. There were a few other Dancers there, at least one who was currently a popular top five warrior, but the twins had been a novelty at their debut working together, neither trying to undercut or kill the other with the Dance seasons only reaffirming their twin bond. The two of them could still draw a crowd

"I am not leaving you, Torri." Tass reached a hand across the round table, to touch her twin's hand. Torri grabbed her hand like they would on the sands. Two necro alarms went off, turning heads towards the tastefully etched aquariums of dirt. They laughed parting hands, sharing impish grins. The alarms died down.

"I know. It's just so far." Torri's said with a sad smile. The scar running down the left side of her face pulling slightly.

"Not far enough!" They both laughed at their common refrain concerning their parental units. "You can both come out and visit once I have the house backup to ship code." Tass said, leaning over the glossy wood table. "No reason to be stuck here when you have a free weekend or week. It is… only a couple hours by hover."

"Very true!" Torri said raising her glass toasting her sister's health.

Dinner was served after the first round of drinks. The meat was grilled, or not to the person's dining preference. Tass ate more vegetables than meat most days. The taste of blood would occasionally send her into a flashback, even this night she had had to put her fork down to drink the heady and sweet Silver wine to rinse the blood taste out from her well done marbled portion of meat.

Torri and Jerico exchanged looks towards the end of dinner, when there were only scraps of the meal left on the plates before them.

Tass took a sip of her wine, savoring the flavor and enjoying the way the pale wine spun in the oversized glasses. The glasses made her small hands seem even smaller. This amused her in a way being slightly inebriated could.

She looked up to her sister and her lover. "Out with it you two," she said with a smile. "Are you finally preggers, sister dear?"

Torri blushed to the roots of her blond hair. "No!" But she did give Jerico a very sweet smile of sharp chiseled pointed white teeth she had not bothered to cap after her Dancing career. "But we are trying," she amended.

"Congratulations!" Tass said with heartfelt love for them both. They could use as much happiness as possible and a child would complete the pair. Possibly four or five.

Jerico tapped Tass on the hand. "That's not what we need to talk about though."

Tass sighed, putting her wine down. "Our oh so lovely parents causing a headache?" Her voice was soft but no less bitter.

"Actually, not this time." Jerico said with a smile he shared with both her and Torri. "When I sat them down and explained that you were taking your life into your own hands and that you had finally written them into your will, they were praising your farming venture."

"Nothing like greed to motivate those two," Tass muttered, deciding a few more sips would do wonders for her frayed nerves.

"Tass, you didn't actually write them in did you?!" Torri was aghast. She leaned forward to start telling her twin the horrors of their parents.

"Pfft. What fool do you think I am? Not even the Witch herself could get me to give them all my money when I die." Tass took a larger than normal sip, coughing slightly. Torri leaned around table to pound her sister on the back.

Tass waived her off. "Fine, fine," she spluttered, putting the wine down. "I did write them into my will, but only for the amount of one ticket to the games."

Torri sat back, her mouth open in both shock and glee. "That's…that's rabid fantastic!" She turned to Jerico. "I need to do that! Tomorrow," she said emphatically.

Jerico picked up her hand and kissed her fingers. His dark hand emphasizing her pale fingers in a lovely way. "Tomorrow we will sit down and re-do your will."

"Thank you love." She gave him a slow kiss that made Tass blush. Torri loved her husband so unabashedly that Tass could not imagine loving anyone not her twin, so deeply. Their parents had broken all of their children in different ways.

"So if you aren't in the mothering way, yet, what is the news?" Tass interrupted the lover birds giggling snuggle fest.

Torri sat up with a deep breath. Tass noticed how she did not let go of Jerico's hand as she fumbled for her purse. She pulled out a rumbled rectangular letter, and actual paper and ink letter, instead of an electronic communication. Torri handed it to her sister almost furtively. "I got this from Titon. You need to read this." Her voice was quiet but it was her eyes that scared Tass. Only when they had to face Titon and Dorigan on the Sands, had Torri had that utter look of rage, desolation, and determination.

Tass took the letter with the care used for one of the Ancient skeletons occasionally found. "Must have cost him a small fortune to send this," was all she said, for the moment, taking a sip of wine examining the paper envelope sealed with electronic tape. The paper was closed with a wax and blood seal. The security of the seals said more than the letter at face value. Tass realized she would rather drink or fight instead of reading what fresh hell he might have to say.

"A friend from work, has a brother who is a ship captain. Two letters were handed over."

"Two?"

"I've already read mine."

"Not three?"

"As far as I know Dorigan won't need or want to know what Titon has to say." Torri took a hasty sip of her almost full glass. "I didn't want to know," she muttered.

"A way off the planet and away from our despised parents would go a long way in saying 'I'm sorry.'" Tass said with the taste of bitter lemon and sand in her mouth thinking of her crippled brother.

"Not when you read what he is doing." Jerico's nostrils flared as his eyes narrowed.

Tass took another sip of wine, her hands not shaking but the floor felt unsteady. She pricked her finger touching the drop of blood to the wax. The wax drank the blood, sending a current through the electronic tape. The tape unsealed, exposing a very thick heavy sheet of paper with only three lines. Expensive, Tori thought scanning the words, her breath huffing out as if he had gut punched her again.

Dear little sister, I could not handle what I was forced to do on the sands. I do my penance with the Runners' God of Justice. I still love you, please forgive me.

In memory, Titon

"Is he fucking insane?!" Tass' voice carried throughout the restaurant. Every head turned towards her. All three risers in the restaurant went off. Jerico reached across the table to put two fingers on her under wrist, the vein pulsing in time with her elevated heart rate and a thumb on top her wrist. The conditioning that calmed all Dancers no matter what flavor worked, but just barely. The risers dirt had exploded with the bones of small creatures erupting from the dirt, muscles, skin and fur flowing over the bleached bones like water in reverse.

One of the Katherian waiters hurried over. It wasn't Torri who stopped him but the other Dancers in the room. Six of them. The stood and waited, tension in the lines of warriors, the necros' held their heads tilted, listening. The other guests stopped eating ready to move out of the way if this became a live Dance.

Tass shook her head but did not shake off Jerico's hand. One breath. Two. The risers stopped screaming. The bones buried themselves in the dirt. Tass slapped the table with her free hand. She was back in control. Jerico let go and the other Dancers sat back down, most just as pleased not to have to fight on their off time. The current warrior glared over his shoulder at Tass for whatever perceived slight to or loss of control by her. The warrior's companion thumped him on the shoulder breaking the glares, whispering something in his ear. A shake of his head and dinner resumed.

Tass swallowed her wine in one large gulp then reached over to take Torri's glass and finishing hers off as well.

"You could have warned me," Tass said hoarsely, a knot in her throat.

"Would you have believed me?" Torri reached a hand across the table.

"No." Tass looked away, but took her sister's hand.

"Our brother needs... something he can't find here."

"Justice isn't what he will get."

"Peace of mind that his death will be agonizing enough perhaps."

Tass looked up, her face draining of blood. "Our parents-"

"Your parents are the only one who will face the consequences of your brother's actions. This is not a reflection on either of you." Jerico's mouth was pressed into a thin line.

"Though when this breaks with the next time Redeyes is seen on the screen and your brother is behind her as one of the Guardians, Torri." Jerico motioned to Torri. "She'll come and visit you for a while until things blow over or your parents are torn to bits on the public's media."

Tass tried to take another sip from her sister's empty glass, failing that she put the glass down with a thump, motioning for their waiter for another bottle. "How bad is this going to be?"

"No Dancer has ever willing worked for the Runners or been forced to be a Guardian."

"But he wasn't forced, now was he?" Tass snapped, flicking the rim of the glass with her finger causing the crystal to chime sweetly in counterpoint to her own emotions.

"No, but that won't change public opinion, who

will assume the worst of your parents." It was Jerico's turn to take a deep breath. "Tass." Jerico tapped Tass' hand catching her attention. "Your parents weren't going to lose any bets no matter who won when they threw all four of their children onto the sands that Dance. They could have protested, keeping you and Torri off the sands or Titon and Dorigan. Either pair of you would have won but they tried to sacrifice all of you for gain not for love. Titon chose to save the two of you after you threw yourself over Torri as Dorigan was about to kill her."

Tass opened her mouth, but Jerico shook his head not letting her speak. "I've watched the films. Dorigan was on a Dancer's high. Nothing mattered anymore to him. Life and death were meaningless. He saw only targets not siblings. You and Torri were both dying and all the bodies from the other Dancers too damaged for either of you to raise for shielding. Titon made his choice. He managed to wake enough to save you both. Dorigan couldn't. Let Titon have this self-sacrifice on his terms."

Tass looked away first. "He'll never be able to come home."

"Would he ever have come home? Really?" Jerico's look penetrated through Tass pipe dreams.

"No." Tass accepted a full glass from the waiter downing half in one sip.

"He sacrificed his win for his sister's life." Jerico's look was as bitter as Tass'. "Not since the Witch and the Warrior has there been so much haranguing over a win. Let him go his path." He squeezed her hand.

Tass, eyes burned. She had long since stopped

complaining about the fairness of life but this time she wanted to be three and have her aunt pick her up and hold her, lying that everything would be fine. She brushed away a tear. "Not much I can do for him. I do wish him well though. The worm bait Goddess is getting a better Guardian than she deserves."

"Yes, yes she is," Torri agreed fervently.

The first night in the new house Tass regretted bringing almost nothing with her but clothes and a small cooler for water in her haste to leave the city.

"You are unprepared girl, how the hell did you survive the Sands?" the old woman's ghost asked as Tass fell through the rotting mattress.

"By summoning cranky old women like you to scare the children," Tass snapped rubbing her bruised bottom. The blanket and sheets little more than dust held together by cobwebs.

Madile snorted as she drifted closer to the blond necromancer. "You're going to need a few more things than this sorry bag of clothing if you want to make a living here."

Tass glared up at the ghost through the broken bed slats. "Why don't you help me figure out a few of those things in the morning?" Acid could burn no sharper.

"Girl, you're going to need someone else to do your thinking if this is the best you got."

"Morning. Until then let me sleep." Tass laid down on the dank thin padding, closing her eyes to huddle under the meager layers of her hastily grabbed clothing.

Tass jerked up as if a hot wire had hit her. "Let me sleep unless there is danger. Watch over me and keep me safe."

The other ghosts drifted out with her command but the old woman nodded approval. "Now you're learning, child."

The Cheshire cat slipped through a broken window pane, the ragged glass merely brushing fur as the cat contorted through a space anyone watching would have sworn was too small for her to move through. Ears twitching and her nose taking in all the new strange scents, led the cat to the room where the new ugly cat with too small a mouth nested. The cat sniffed as the smell triggered a memory. The cat sniffed again. Same scent as previous without any extra ugly cats.

The hairless cat opened its eyes, slowly blinking, much like a newborn kitten. The squeak was definitely kitten like. The Cheshire stretched out her neck to sniff a little closer. The dust from the nesting material caused the cat to sneeze profusely. The ugly kitten started to thrash in its bedding throwing soft not plant things around in agitation. The Cheshire looked for tails and ears. The ears were deformed and the tail nonexistent. The Cheshire shook her head in pity, before wandering out to explore more of the odd ugly kitten's den.

"What in a nova's corona is that?!" Tass squeaked. The feline head had a smile that almost reached her ears with sharp pointy teeth filling the mouth from end to end. The long blue striped animal sneezed and turned back around with no more than a glance at Tass and a shake of its head.

"Eh, That's the Cheshire that lives here. Easy going enough, helps take down the frog population." Madile said dismissively. "As long as you don't mess with her kittens, she'll leave you alone. Feed the damn things and you'll never get rid of them or able to keep chickens."

"I knew they were big but that was... But it won't bite or attack?" Tass stood slowly gathering the clothes she wore for warmth that were now scattered.

"Mess with its food and children, it will. Give it room and it will clear out the small varmints you'll have running around," Madile said slowly as if to a young child.

"Ok." Tass was skeptical but ghosts didn't lie to her. She laid back down trying to gather sleep around her, but morning light was already creeping in through the window.

"Hey Miok! Going to see the new owner of the old Madile place. Want to come with?" Joshin asked his pale skinned blond brother.

Miok put down the hoe, considering the rows done, weighing his options carefully. Mom would bust his ass if the work weren't done but his dad was a little more laid back. "If we're back before sunset so I can get the last three rows done, sure," He said with a shrug of a wiry shoulder. Joshin laughed at his ship twin brother.

The boys were less than ten months apart, both 19. Joshin looked more like their mother, short dark skinned with amber eyes, broad in the shoulders but Joshin was still underweight, by a good 40 lbs. Miok took after their father. Tall blond, wiry. He too needed to fill in the hollows that muscular definition showed off, little of what he had was padding. The way the boys ate though you had to wonder where they put the food if not into muscle.

"Hollow legs," was all their laconic father would say. Their mom had a few more choice words, sharp but was always with affection.

"Let's go!" Joshin grabbed a helmet from the rack tossing one to his brother and grabbing the second for himself. Their dirt bikes were respectable only in the sense the frames were metal and the solar charges un-cracked. Everything was jury rigged and hand built, with raw welded seams and dents in weird places from dropped hammers or tractor jacks. The farm did well with selling exotic flowers, but their father insisted the boys know how to build anything from scratch first before asking for the latest gadgets.

The boys had become self-reliant in many ways. Miok had built their home computer system from parts bought in town while Joshin got the equipment and sprinklers working no matter how corroded in rust the original scrap-yard pieces were.

Their parents loved their dedication, but despaired that neither had the love for farming their dad did. Those in town were want to joke that Kivans could put a twig in the dirt and have a forest ready for harvest in two months, while his wife Mia was the brains behind the business, getting the best contracts for their floral and hemp harvests. Mia may have been a Dancer for three seasons, but her true calling was riding herd on her husband and two boys, while keeping the business running smoothly.

Miok could hear the voices as they hit the rarely used washed out gravel and dirt road, the closer they got to old Madile's place. A murmur at first, that grew into a muted conversation drawing him in. He didn't remember standing his bike up or walking into the house. He walked into a conversation between old Madile and a living petite blond girl.

"No, I don't want to keep the walls completely closed in. We need light in here." The blonde was saying crossly to the ghost of an old woman.

"You're going to knock out supporting walls." The ghost was pointing at walls where three zombies stood with sledge hammers.

"Arches and windows are what this place needs!"

"Not with those damn frogs around! You'll have them through those ground windows in quicksand minute."

"Look old woman-"

"She's right." Miok said interrupting the living woman and the ghost. "The frogs will come through the lower windows looking for fresh meat. Which would be you."

The blond glared at him, covered in dust and plaster, gripping a crowbar tightly between two bleeding white knuckled fists.

"And who are you, boy, to be telling us how to do

this?" Madile asked, her voice waspish at being interrupted.

"I'm Miok. I live down the road a bit," Miok said, waving a hand towards home's general direction.

The ghost tilted her head. "I don't hear nothing. No ghosts in your family. You must be new."

"Our family came out here with my mom's stake from the Dance with my dad a few years back," Miok said proudly.

"She a necro?" the blond asked.

"Warrior." The girl cringed slightly at this but held her stance.

"I see your brother." Madile snapped with pale pursed lips. "Dark as night."

"He takes after her."

"You?"

"My dad and I could have been twins at this age."

Madile humphed but said nothing more.

"Brother? I don't see anyone here but Miok," the girl said irritably, trying to brush hair out of her eyes, pushing more plaster into sweat soaked hair.

"Joshin." Miok turned to look behind him. He didn't see his brother either. "He was right behind me."

"He's trying to get your attention." Madile said. "Well he was. He's gone off now."

"Why would he leave?" Miok was mildly concerned, though not enough to leave.

"Kids. Who knows." Madile turned back to the blond. "Ok girl. You can have the windows but you have to have something over them or you'll be dead in a week's time once the frogs figure out there is something young and tasty here!"

"I have double paned security glass. Nothing less than a 6-inch disc from a railgun, that are ONLY supported by Guardian vehicles, is getting through that," she said click her teeth together, chewing her words.

"What the hell do you need glass that thick for? Expecting a God through those windows?" the ghost rolled her eyes at the girl.

"Yes. This area is rife with the dead from the first settlement. Not human and void raping stronger than any human dead around." the blonde said with exasperation, putting a hand on hip, gesturing with the crowbar. "My nightmares could possibly raise one and I wanted to make sure any windows would hold up to them trying to get through!"

"Why do you want windows then, you need metal walls?!" The two circled back to stylized difference.

"For light during the day and I want to see the stars at night! Now let me get the windows into place old woman." The exasperation was palatable with exchanged glares.

"You know Madile is dead, right? You could just tell her to butt out," Miok said watching the two verbally spar with a fascination.

"She needs me willing to work with her. And telling me to go hang won't get her the information she really wants." The ghost was smug, crossing smoky outlined arms over an ample if just as smoky bosom.

"She's a necro. She can make you do anything." It was Miok's turn to roll his eyes.

"She can make me do anything true but information can be held back to really fuck up a person or an expedition. In this case farming, the girl here has never gotten her hands buried in dirt before."

The blond looked at the ghost sourly. "I need her willing to help me farm this place for Kopi berries."

Miok whistled. "Kopi berries are like finding gold nuggets in frog shit. Rare and dangerously hard to get."

The old ghost cackled rubbing her ethereal hands together. "Exactly, and I grew the best when alive."

"Hence co-operative," the girl said rolling her eyes. "There will be windows and the frogs will be dealt with as they come."

"You going Hunting?"

"Nope. Dancing. All these bodies around here can be raised to hunt 'em if they decide to come to me."

"Now that's what I like to hear. Damn frogs use to take up more time trying to defend the house then all the farming put together. Put your windows in girl and keep the dead close!" Madile cackled rubbing long dead hands together energetically.

Miok was going to say more when he was violently pulled out of dead space by two fingers and a thumb on his wrist.

Joshin watched his brother put the bike's kickstand down and walk into the house as if he owned it. No knocking, no calling who he was.

"Miok! We don't live here you can't just walk in like that."

Miok ignored him letting the door close behind him on rusted screeching springs. Joshin followed him in. The interior of the house was as messy as the exterior. Zombies had pulled down siding with windows partially pulled out connected only by the bottom sill, with more zombies still holding the windows in. There were nine zombies that Joshin counted in the living room. All had stopped. The living room smelled of plaster, dirt and old leather.

Miok stopped a few feet from a petite blond. Like the zombies Miok didn't move. He breathed and stared at a space mid-way between the kitchen and the living room.

"Miok!" Joshin yelled, then snapped fingers in front of his brother's eyes. Miok didn't track Joshin's fingers or anything else. "What the hell, brother." Joshin slapped his brother once, then again. The same results as snapping fingers. Nothing.

"Dead lost," Joshin breathed, adrenaline spiking along his skin making his heart race. "Damn it. Now I'm going to have to get mom and she's going to skin us both alive!"

Joshin ran for his bike watching the setting sun. He didn't think the frogs would be out tonight, but he had to get his mom before nightfall either way. He wasn't going to leave his brother lost talking to the dead in an unprotected house.

Mia's dark skin was a deep blue black with hues of purple in the afternoon soon, contrasting against her husband's pale arms. She stared up into his eyes with a lingering smile.

"What are you laughing at woman?" Kivans said with a smile, looking deeply into her eyes.

"That I caught myself the best man out there," she teased, giving him a kiss.

He savored that kiss, turning pink along his cheeks. "Flattery will get you everything," was all he said, pulling her close.

"And the truth?" Mia asked tilting her head coquettishly.

"Even more!" He pulled her in for another kiss.

A racing motorbike was heard in the background at the edge of the city as the bike shifted down hard, grinding gears.

"Someone's looking to break their bike with that kind of abuse," Kivans said, breaking off from kissing his wife, with a frown,

Mia looked towards the sound, making out the dust covered figure. "That's our son!"

"Not both?" Kivans looked past the one bike waiting for the other bike to appear at the end of the street.

"No." They both turned towards the racing bike down main street waiting. Mia felt a knot of fear in her belly draw tight. The boys never went anywhere without the other.

The bike squealed to a stop next to them. "Joshin! What the..." Kivans started on a blistering reprimand.

"Mom! Miok is at Madile's old place. Dead lost. I can't wake him!" Joshin stared at his mother, frantically, talking over his dad.

Mia and Kivans exchanged glances. She handed

her husband the mail and the full hemp woven grocery bag. "Get to the house and bring the guns. I'm not going to make it to Madile's place before nightfall."

Kivans nodded, understanding. They'd had a few run ins with a couple of frog hunting parties in the past few weeks. The frog bodies had taken two days to burn. Luckily their neighbors were in the same boat but the stench lingered still. Night was their prime time, and summer their most active as they gathered food for the winter.

She swung up behind Joshin. "Go."

"Helmet?"

"Now child!" she snapped, poking him in the ribs, with enough force he'd have a bruise on his dark skin tomorrow. "Just don't wreck us and we'll be good."

The sun was setting fast. Joshin took the dirt and gravel roads at an almost reckless speed. He didn't dare cut across the fields. To many ditches hidden by thigh high weeds, sometimes spiked by the frogs for unwary prey driven into their traps.

They got to Madile's house just as the last liquid gold of the sun fell below the horizon. The air hot and heavy from the day, giving only a slight promise with a breeze for a cooler evening.

Joshin skidded his bike along the gravel road, bracing with one booted foot. The action violent enough to startled the purple and blue Cheshire from her spot in the front yard tree. The cat bounded into the high grass at this noisy invasion, growling in protest at the intrusion of her territory.

Mia jumped off from behind. Not as flexible as

when she was a Dancer but still athletic enough to vault from back of the pieced together bike, bounding up the stairs, shouting over her shoulder "Grab anything you can swing just in case we have a hunting party incoming!"

Joshin parked the bike on the side of the house then pulled Miok's there. He scrounged for usable weapons, finding 3-inch metal poles six feet long. He flexed the rusted pole testing for weakness. The pole bent but didn't break. No telling how old but it would do for a pole arm. Another pole broke into two pieces. These pieces his mother could use. She could use a blade of grass and a twig and come out ahead of anyone he knew in a fight, Miok thought wryly.

"Joshin! Joshin!" Mia called for her oldest son as she rushed through the screen door. She saw the zombies, motionless and waiting then her son next to Tass. She skidded to a halt. Both her son and the necromancer were looking at a point in the living room. Both breathed slowly and steadily, blinking every other minute. Dead stuck.

"Damn it, boy. You weren't supposed to be able to talk to the dead!" Mia vented into the empty air. She stepped on the safe side of her son, taking his wrist between the first two fingers of her hand and thumb. Counting with his pulse she pressed hard every other beat. He didn't come out of the thrall. She wrapped her hand around his wrist, taking the more direct approach and more dangerous, yanking him off his feet and into her body.

Joshin hadn't been prepared for being stuck in a death loop nor for seeing his mother next to him.

The living room gathered shadows as daylight faded.

"Mom? What... time is it?"

"We're leaving now." Mia pulled on her son. They both heard something like thunder but wasn't getting closer. Frog drums.

"No! We can't leave the girl." He turned back to Tass reaching for her. Mia slapped his hand away hard.

"Mom! What the space was that the for?" He cradled his hand, now red from her slap, to his chest. The zombies turned to look at the mother and her son. The motion not wasted on Mia.

"Never try to yank a necro out of a death loop if you aren't trained," she said through gritted teeth. "Go stand by the door. No, matter what do NOT interrupt!"

Mia sat on her knees, her lips moving a prayer to the Death. She reached a hand up to cradle the girl's limp wrist in a gentle grip. The zombies didn't move towards her or Joshin. Mia tightened her grip. Pulsing with the girl's heartbeat. The zombies moved towards them.

"Come on girl! Wake out of it!" Mia kept her voice light, a bead of sweat rolled down her forehead. The zombies took a step towards Mia then another. The drums were getting louder, closer.

"Wake up!" Mia hissed.

Tass blinked, then blinked again. The zombies stopped mid stride. Two fell over.

Tass flinched but only said "I'm here," to the kneeling woman.

"About time, girl!" Mia stood with a stretch,

popping her neck. "We got other things to do now that you're out of dead suck! Them frogs will be headin' over so get your zombies on perimeter duty. Now girl! Hustle!"

Tass just stared at the woman. "Who are you? And why are you here?"

"The frogs are coming, girl." Mia put her hands on her hips, giving a slight shake of her head at the former Dancer.

Miok stepped forward noting Tass' discomfort. "Mom, this is Tass. The necromancer who bought Madile's old farm." Miok turned to Tass. "Tass, I'd like you to meet my mother. She was a Dancer…"

Recognition dawned in Tass's face. She sucked in a breath, speaking in a husky voice. "She Danced over 20 years ago with the best knife throwing record and hamstringing to ever survive. An inside fighter," Tass said, holding out her hand slowly to the other woman.

Mia's lips twitched. "You weren't alive back then to watch me Dance."

"My brothers watched your old fights. Every inside fighter studies your moves. And if you're a fighter counting on range to keep you safe, you study how to keep the inside fighters outside of their range and at your own."

Mia flashed a wide smile. "Good to know, these old bones contributed something."

Drums cut across the conversation. Close, sharp, reverberating along Tass' skin.

"Space!" Joshin swore, tossing his mother the broken end of rebar. The other one he kept for himself. There was a sputtering roar distant in the background.

"Your father's here, which will even out the odds a little," Mia said grimly, facing the open window frames.

A long sinuous shape grumbled her way in. All four of the living turned to look at the Cheshire cat that slunk in. The cat glared at the four humans as if they were responsible for the influx of frogs. She let out a hiss, before sauntering up the wide stairs.

The four looked at each other, then the retreating cat.

"I think she's got the right idea," Tass said.

"Up, up!" Mia said making a shooing motion to the three. "Girl. Tass, you got the undead around the house?"

"I'll need a moment to pull a few more."

"We'll give you the time. Make sure they know to take the heads or the damn things'll regenerate everything else."

Tass let her eyes, glaze over slightly "feeling" with a light touch for the undead. In an unconscious gesture from her days on the Sands, she stuck out her left hand, reaching for her twin. Miok responded by reaching for her hand, when Mia yanked it down.

"No. You're not trained and this ain't a training session." Mia looked him square in the eye. "Later the girl can teach you how to pull the dead or anything else but not tonight."

"Yes, mom," was all Miok said looking between her and Tass, though the burning curiosity couldn't be hidden behind his pale honey brown eyes.

Tass pulled the close ones. There were four more in the graveyard that responded and another two outside of the house graveyard. These two wanted to fight. They're souls hadn't moved on and they hated still, ready for violence. Tass bound them tightly to her will not letting them stray from her command. The others were non-ensouled bodies, needing only her directions

"Ahh. I see you found the Miller twins," Madile said, ghostly pale that all could hear and see, with Tass flexing her necromancy.

"You know them?" Mia asked. "They been missing for over 62 years."

"Know them? Child, I put them in those graves for a ship raping reason." Madile snorted. "They'll make good frog killers."

Mia gave the ghost a shocked look but went back to the windows.

Tass felt something else. A stirring of something large. Like the dangerous twins this one also felt ensouled. Emotions whispered in a death wrapped sleep. The strongest being hunger not hate, though depending on what it was hungry for, the distinction could be minimal. Tass pulled back her summons from that... one. She felt a slight questioning twinge as it sleepily settled back into the dark.

"I've pulled all I can," Tass said, turning back to her unusual fighting team.

"Girl, I hope you're as good here as you were on the sands," Mia growled, "those frogs are coming and it looks like the have their whole village."

"How many?"

"Over 80 plus warriors with another 200 for cleaning and gleaning."

Tass gave Mia a wide smile. "Give me some bodies and I'll add them to my collection. We've got this!"

Mia shook her head praying to the Gods that the girl hadn't gone insane already.

To find out more about S.R. Ruark and her books, visit
www.indiesunited.net/sr-ruark

SUSPENSE

Dead on Time

Guy Thair

"Is anyone sitting here?"

Bailey looked up from the crossword he was working on, shading his eyes from the low evening sun as he squinted at the silhouetted figure above him, "No, be my guest."

"Thank you," said the newcomer, seating himself opposite Bailey, extending one hand and dropping keys, coins, and other pocket debris onto the street cafe's small table with the other, "Dennis Opperman, pleased to meet you."

"Hello," Bailey shook the man's hand and nodded, then began to clear a space on the table, moving his folded newspaper and placing it on the third, unoccupied chair, "a very pleasant evening to sit and watch the world go by."

"It is indeed, I'm rather fond of this spot myself. Are you from out of town, I've not seen you here before?"

"No, no I've been around for a while, just don't get across town too often, that's all."

"Hey Guido," Opperman clicked his fingers loudly a few times in the direction of a waiter, as he hurried past with a tray loaded with plates, "can I get some service here?"

The waiter shot him a withering look and carried the clattering pile into the cafe, reappearing a few moments later with menu and a notepad.

"The special today is roasted tomato and basil tart with…"

"Just a coffee," Bailey's uninvited guest abruptly interrupted the young man, "and bring me an ashtray."

"A coffee and an ashtray, of course, sir. Nothing to eat?"

"Are you deaf? I said just coffee."

"Right you are sir, no ashtray then?"

Opperman, instantly furious, turned to glare at the waiter, "Are you taking the piss boy?"

"Not at all sir, just checking," he smirked, I'll be right back."

"Bloody cheeky little sod, no respect these days," he gave Bailey an expectant look, "don't you think?"

"Oh I don't know, most young people seem quite polite, I've certainly found they respond well to good manners anyway."

The sarcasm seemed to pass Opperman by completely.

"You got kids then?" he asked Bailey, clearly uninterested in the answer and absently patting his pockets as if looking for something

"I haven't, no," Bailey replied, "not anymore." He watched the other man searching his pockets once more before inquiring, "Have you lost something?"

"Can't find my damn cigarettes, sure I had them with me earlier." He began the search for the third time.

"Here, have one of mine," said Bailey, passing an open packet across the table, "I'm trying to cut down anyway."

"Yeah? Forty-a-day man myself and never even had a cold," he reached out and snatched the proffered cigarette, "a load of bollocks they talk about it giving you cancer, all part of the government's programme of brainwashing, you mark my words." He flicked a cheap lighter and drew heavily on the cigarette, blowing the smoke carelessly across the table as the waiter returned and unceremoniously dumped a tray in front of Opperman.

"Your coffee and ashtray, sir," he said, "will there be anything else?"

"No. And don't expect a tip either," Opperman snapped, as the waiter turned to leave, raising his eyebrows at Bailey, who smiled and shook his head in silent agreement with the young man, whose name badge read "Kevin", and his obvious opinion of the obnoxious customer, "In fact wait, I've changed my mind. Bring me a double brandy will you."

"Is that the house brandy sir?" asked Kevin politely.

"No, I don't want any of that cheap shit, the good stuff boy, that's what I'm after." He watched the waiter depart and then turned back to Bailey, "Did you see that little bastard was talking back to me again?"

"I'm sure he didn't mean anything by it Dennis, he's probably had a long day, we all have. I expect it's the heat. A young lad like that, run off his feet all day in this weather, he's probably exhausted."

"Crap!" he slapped his hand on the table, making the cups jump in their saucers, "They need to toughen up a bit, these kids nowadays. I've been at my desk since eight this morning, ten o'clock I had to take a load of clients for drinks, then to lunch, I had to stop for a pint with a couple of blokes from head office after work and now," he paused, took one final, ferocious drag on the cigarette, before crushing it out in the ashtray," now I've got to drive halfway across town in this fucking traffic…" he trailed off and looked up, as Kevin returned and placed a large brandy glass on the table in front of him.

Opperman raised a hand to indicate he should wait, drained the glass and slammed it back down on the table.

"So I'll be wanting another one of those…" he focused his unsteady gaze on the waiter's badge, "…Kevin. Go on boy, chop-chop, hop to it!"

"Are you sure you should be driving Dennis?" asked Bailey, still smiling but sounding concerned, "You don't look so good you know."

"Rubbish, I can take my booze better than anyone I know!" becoming aggressive now, he snatched the glass from the tray as Kevin was cautiously approaching the table, seemingly not noticing the brandy that slopped on his sleeve and down his shirt as he threw back the remainder in one gulp, "Right lot of bloody nancy boys these days, I could drink the whole fucking lot of 'em under the table!"

Opperman grabbed another cigarette, blearily glancing at Bailey as he did so, "You don't mind, right? Trying to cut down, you said."

"No, not at all Dennis, feel free," said Bailey cheerfully, "one or two more or less won't make any difference now anyway."

Denis Opperman scrabbled amongst the detritus of his pockets, spread out on the cluttered table, until he located his lighter, managing to light the cigarette on the fourth attempt and collapsed heavily back into his chair, sweating profusely, with an expression of puzzlement.

"Legs feel a bit strange, think I'd better sit for a while," he wheezed, "don't know what's come over me. Must be the heat, like you said."

"Oh, I'm pretty sure it's not just the heat. Not just the booze either I'm afraid, although I'm sure you've drunk enough to make most people keel over, so congratulations on that. No, I'm afraid your problem is somewhat more... terminal than that."

He let Opperman, who was now giving Bailey his undivided attention, absorb his words before he continued, "Because you see Denis, I know who you are, even if I mean nothing to you, like my daughter's life didn't, I know all about you."

Opperman now looked panicky, almost terrified, and yet he remained sitting in the chair across from this stranger that he'd met only thirty minutes earlier, staring as though transfixed, his mouth moving silently, his eyes darting this way and that as if searching for a way out. Then he seemed to come to his senses and addressed Bailey in a strangled voice.

"Your daughter? I don't understand, you said you didn't have kids."

"I said that I didn't have children anymore," replied Bailey, his expression, previously friendly, had turned as hard as stone now, all amusement gone from his eyes, "my daughter was taken from me exactly a year ago today," he looked at his watch, "in twenty minutes in fact. Then it will be precisely a year, to the minute, since a hit and run driver ran down my daughter as she walked home from her friend's house. Police say he must have mounted the pavement, more than likely drunk, going way over the speed limit. Deborah never stood a chance. That was her name Dennis; Deborah. I thought you should know that before you died."

Opperman's eyes bulged desperately, but he seemed unable to get his voice to work anymore, his mouth opened and closed like a dying goldfish.

"Allow me to fill in a few details for you Dennis," said Bailey, "just so you don't miss anything important," he glanced at his watch again, "although I'd better hurry, we don't have long, or should I say, you don't." his smile of satisfaction at Opperman's increasing discomfort was no more than a grimace now, as he turned his blazing eyes on the terrified man and continued in a voice devoid of emotion.

"You were driving back from a meeting with some high-class clients at the time Dennis. Had a few bottles of bubbly to celebrate closing the deal."

Opperman's eyes rolled wildly, his body otherwise

frozen in the chair but his distress was plainly visible nonetheless.

Bailey continued in the same steady, emotionless tone, "On the phone to your mistress when you killed Debbie weren't you? Didn't even bother to stop and call for help. Don't bother denying it, I've seen your phone records, I've seen your self-pitying e-mails. Oh, I'm sorry, you can't deny it can you? Don't worry, we'll come to that in a minute," the humorless grin again, "Do you know, I've spent the last year getting to know you very well indeed, Dennis Opperman. Where you work, where you live and, most importantly, where you drink. Here, for instance," Bailey tapped the table with a fingertip, "I've noticed you like to get drunk and abuse the unfortunate staff here on a Friday after you finish work and before then driving home, hence my surprise appearance at your usual table this fine evening."

Opperman's face managed to convey bewilderment but little else, so Bailey spoke once more.

"Oh look here, I've found your cigarettes for you, I must have picked them up with my paper." Bailey lifted the newspaper off the chair beside him to reveal Opperman's crumpled packet and indicated his pack, still lying where Opperman had left them, after taking the second one a few moments before, "and, this is the part that I feel sure will interest you Dennis; you've been smoking these," he picked up the packet, to show there were only two missing, "and I'm afraid I added a little something to them."

He let that sink in, watching Opperman's mouth working listlessly, his eyes staring madly at Bailey. "I'm a chemist you see, a pharmacist by trade, I have access to all sorts of fascinating compounds, several of which are now circulating through your bloodstream. One of them is responsible for your current state of immobility whilst another is interfering with your speech. But most of them are concentrating on your nervous system and internal organs, all of which will soon begin shutting down for good. There is literally nothing you can do. A sensation I have become only too familiar with over the past year, but one which I believe will begin to fade very, very soon."

He picked up the newspaper, glanced briefly at Opperman, eyelids starting to droop now, consulted his watch one last time and returned to the final unsolved clue in his interrupted crossword; "Relieving traumatic experiences through emotional closure". Bailey thought for a moment, nodded, filled in the small white squares with a wry smile and left the newspaper folded so Opperman could see it. Then he got up, left Kevin a large tip and walked into the bustling crowd.

In the last moments of Denis Opperman's life, peering at the paper through the rapidly closing tunnel of his fading vision, he could just make out the word, " Catharsis".

To find out more about Guy Thair and his books, visit
www.indiesunited.net/guy-thair

NONFICTION

Ethical Objectivity

Dr. Sanford W. Wood, PhD

I think most of us want to believe that our ethical principles are objective. It would be comforting to say, like Jefferson, that they are the laws of nature and of nature's god. Maybe we are not inclined to call them the laws of nature, but we would like to believe that they exist. But if they do exist, *where* do they exist? In philosophical terms, what is their ontological status? It is my considered opinion that they have none.

To put it another way, I believe that ethical knowledge is not possible, in the sense of knowing ethical facts. We can know facts *about* ethics, such as anthropological or historical knowledge about people's ethical beliefs in times past. We can also know sociological facts about people's ethical beliefs in different societies, and psychological facts about the correlation (if any) between certain personality types and the person's ethical beliefs. But we can never know ethical facts as such because there are no such facts to know.

This means that our ethical beliefs are never

justified. I can attempt to explain to someone how I came to believe as I do about something, but that is an explanation, not a justification. It doesn't mean that my belief is justified in the sense of being objectively correct.

What about Jefferson's other possibility, that our ethical beliefs are the laws of God? This is a legitimate possibility, and I don't want to dismiss it out of hand. But in my mind, this raises the question of *why* they are God's laws. Does God choose them because they are right, or are they right because God chooses them? If God chooses them because they are right, then we are back to the original question about their objective existence. If they are right because God chooses them, then we have avoided my problem but at a terrible price. I don't see any logical problem with believing that ethical principles are entirely arbitrary, depending upon the will of God. Just let me say that I would not want to believe in such a god.

If ethical principles are not objective, what is their status? My thesis is that we just make them up. I don't mean to sound frivolous. And I certainly don't think we have a license to run amok. If anything, we have a greater burden of responsibility, because not only am I responsible for doing the right thing; I am also responsible for determining what the right thing is.

Let me say, before going any further down this road, that I don't think I can prove my thesis. Indeed, after many years of thinking about things philosophical, I don't think there's much that I *can* prove. So humor an old man for a few minutes, while

I share my thoughts with you, for what they're worth.

Let me hasten to say that we are not gods. We do not create ethical standards *ex nihilo*. We all have an ethical heritage derived from various sources: family, friends, faith, and society at large. And we can just accept that heritage uncritically, as most people do, or we can reflect on it and determine what to accept and what to change.

I want to talk a bit about the role of moral heroes. These are people of outstanding character who impress us by their examples and inspire us to imitate them. And they don't have to be real. We may be inspired by a novelist's creation of a fictitious person of such exemplary character that we feel inspired to imitate them. We should not neglect the role of emotion in ethics. Our ethical principles should not be dispassionate beliefs. Rather, they should inspire us to act. I suppose my principal objection to utilitarianism is more emotional than logical. It seems to cheapen morality by reducing it to a cost-benefit analysis.

I think that living an ethical life is not a matter of following rules of behavior. I think it is more like pursuing an ideal. What kind of person do I want to be? What kind of society do I want to live in? More often than not, this is an ideal pursued in the negative: Am I ashamed of what I have done? Even if I can get away with it, have I in the process become the kind of person I would not want as a friend?

Let us briefly consider the role of wisdom. It is not the same as strength of character. A man can be wise in the sense of being able to make good choices in morally complex situations, but not have the moral fortitude to pursue his choices. A part of wisdom is the ability to evaluate people and situations, and some people are better at it than others. Just as some people are better at grading apples than others are, you can improve with practice. You rarely hear of a wise young person. Some people make this difference by distinguishing between intellectual and moral virtues. Thus, wisdom would be an intellectual virtue, courage a moral virtue.

There are many facets to the moral life, but if I had to summarize it for me, it is the pursuit of nobility of character. One of the reasons that I am attracted to the Christian faith is because of the Christian moral vision. But that's a story for another day.

To find out more about Dr. Sanford W Wood and his books, visit
www.indiesunited.net/sanford-wood

HUMOROUS NONFICTION

Things They Never Warned Me About

Lisa Orban

Watching my own children have children of their own has been a fun experience for me, much to their dismay. When they come to me with some new 'horror' story of parenting looking for my support, I have to say, the urge not to laugh is often overwhelming as I try to be somber and supportive for them. But I vividly remember those days of their childhood as I desperately tried to keep my sanity as they did their best to find new and inventive ways to make me lose it. So, enjoy these snapshots of my insanity while raising my children. And for all those parents out there, know you are not alone, we've all been there.

No one ever told me about all the things I would lose after I had children. I was told about the joys of motherhood, the deep sense of accomplishment I would feel, the unbridled love that I would have for this unformed human being, but of the things I would lose; never. I was never informed that at some point after I had children that I would completely lose my mind. That somehow, all small children have the ability to take a rational, intelligent person and turn their minds into oatmeal. No one ever mentioned that one day I would lock myself in my bedroom to stomp my feet, shake my head, and throw a tantrum that would have impressed my three-year-old had he seen it.

I was completely unprepared to lose my figure, my fashion sense, and the ability to brush my hair with any degree of accuracy. I've had a busy day, you know; my children have learned to walk, talk and climb, and each day was filled with a new and unexpected adventure in motherhood. I would like to have dinner ready on the table each night, and the house clean and orderly, instead I'm rushing to and fro, frantically chasing my children through the house, desperately trying to bathe them before bedtime and not bring the layers of grime they had accumulated through an eventful evening in the garden pulling up my flowers into their beds.

I had once been a smart and funny person with an expansive vocabulary and decent social skills, I was never warned I would be dealing with children whose entire vocabulary was the word "mine!" and a complete unwillingness to compromise with any reasonable request made by their sibling. My light humor and engaging conversational skills were completely lost on these small beings that ran amok in my house and left trails of food and clothing for me to follow like Hansel and Gretel through this new and uncharted territory I was wandering through.

I was never warned that stupid things would just

fall from my mouth like water from a faucet and I would be completely helpless to stop them. "Take the cat in the hat back in the house right now!" I would demand of my daughter, and she obliged me enough to pick up the cowboy hat she had put one of our kittens in and take it back in the house. "Take that apple out of your ear right now!" Then watch my child start to cry while pulling apple chunks out of the wrong orifice. Who says these things? Obviously, I do, but must these comments come so frequently?

I was never informed that the only thing worse than my children fighting was them getting along, as I discovered one day while walking into my bathroom to find my 8-year-old son cutting my 4-year-old daughter's hair because he was trying to be nice, and she wanted to play "beauty parlor". Or the day my older daughter offered to watch my younger daughter in the bathtub so I could answer the phone, and she climbed into the tub with her so they could tie-dye themselves with my make-up, just because it sounded like fun.

I wasn't prepared to walk through the perilous pitfalls of puberty with my sons, and then find out later it's a completely different set of parameters for girls. I was never warned that one day I would roam through my house with a hammer and screwdriver taking every door off its hinge so I would never again have to hear one of my teenagers slam a door shut. I did leave the bathroom door, if you're interested, but it was a close call.

Nor was I ever told about how to deal with the sense of loss I would feel when first one child, and then another leaves, or how to stand at my son's wedding and watch my baby boy stand by his new wife, preparing to start their own life together. I wasn't prepared when I began to cry over the loss of dirty hands on my clean walls, and towels hanging unperturbed on their hooks, of doors back on their hinges and all cats accounted for in the house. As I watched my children leave the house one by one, I thought to myself, I could share these things with them, warn them of the pitfalls and perils of parenthood before they became parents themselves, but then I paused. Nah. Why would I want to spoil the fun for them?

To find out more about Lisa Orban and her books, visit
www.indiesunited.net/lisa-orban

LITERARY FICTION

Willy's Tavern
Madison, Wisconsin
April 1973

Michael Deeze

The old man sat on his bar stool looking at me in the mirror behind the bar. Two empty shot glasses sit between the two half-filled beer glasses on the bar. Even when I was very young, he was an old man. This man I've known my whole life. To me he hasn't aged a day, a constant in the swirling winds of my life. His speech has always been slow and considered, his movements—the same. Today he has something on his mind and I know that when he's ready he'll get around to it. When Thomas Quinn had something to say, the people in my family listened.

Willy's Tavern has been another constant in my life. Just around the corner from both the Quinn and Casey homeplaces, it's close enough to walk to and stagger home from. I've been coming to Willy's as long as I can remember, the sights and smells of it as familiar as my grandmother's house. As a small boy, the Casey and Quinn men repaired to Willy's every

144

Saturday afternoon, leaving the house to the women. At Willy's they spent long hours nursing their beer glasses, eating pickled eggs and pig's feet and staring at themselves in this same mirror behind the bar, all of them friends, but only to each other. The young men and boys came with, playing the juke box and drinking six-ounce Coca Colas with the nickels, sparingly supplied by their uncles.

I grew up watching Willy, a cigarette dangling from the corner of his mouth, pour shots and tap beers while in constant conversation. Willy was always friendly with a wide smile but he also enforced the peace when it was necessary, with a bung starter or the sawed-off he kept handy under the bar. No matter how late the men came home on Saturday night, Willy Donovan would still be in his regular church pew on Sunday up at St. Pat's dressed in the same green tie and jacket. Willy's Tavern was Thomas' go-to place when it was time to hand out advice and wisdom.

When we had arrived, Willy smiled big and after wiping his hands on his apron, leaned across the counter and shook my hand congratulating me on my return home. He proudly showed me where my name and picture were posted on the wall above the liquor bottles; my brother Andy, a Marine, next to me. Ours weren't the only pictures, there were several, each with a small red and white pendant and a blue star in the center. Two of the stars were gold, a testament to the price of heroism. Without being asked Willy had set up the glasses and reached high up for the good whiskey, the first one on the house.

We're into our second shot now, and the first beer is moving toward the finish line. Thomas is warming up. We've already covered the "What are your plans" topic, and the "How do you like your job", as well as how is your mother? and what is Kate up to these days. It strikes me that this man may be the most respected person I know. I recognize how privileged I am to occupy a seat next to him; or to even know him. With a wave, Thomas signals Willy to pour three more, and when they arrive he hands one to Willy and then turns, handing me the second.

"Here's to the miles under your boots, and to the blessing of your return to us. It is too long since the last time you sat on that stool, welcome home Emmett, we're proud to welcome you home safe. Slainte!"

"Slainte, and by the Saints" solemnly spoken by Willy.

"Slainte Seanathair"

Willy threw back his shot and slammed the glass upside down on the bar, gave me a wink and moved off to the other end, where he turned up the volume on the old television, and began rearranging the bottles under it. Even Willy knows that now it's time and with a deep breath Thomas begins, "They came home different as well you know."

"They?"

"Your uncles...and Mick."

"You mean when they came home after the war?"

"Yeah, they were changed by it, all of them. And you are too. It shows; you've become more *careful*."

"It's not the same Grandpa."

"It is exactly the same. Don't you see?"

"You mean, like they say, the Army "makes a man out of you."

"The Army can't make a man out of anyone. That's just bullshit. The man finds out what kind of man he is maybe, but the man himself makes the man. The Army just gives him the environment to find out if he's got the stomach and the spine to do it."

I fished out a cigarette out of my shirt pocket, the match shook a little while I lit it. Thomas Quinn was one of the few men I'd never been able to bullshit, he could skewer me right here on this bar stool and I'd have to tell the truth.

"All the same, it's different. World War II was to save the world, and they came home heroes, all of them. This was a completely different thing altogether."

"You should ask them about it you know."

"Ask who? Little Mick? No offense Grandpa but he's not the easiest guy to talk to when he likes you. He doesn't have the time of day for me."

"Your Da holds up his end of the conversation, when there's conversation worth having."

A pause and another sip of beer. I took the moment to go back through the years, to when I was a kid and all of the boys talked about their dads, and uncles, and the war. When we played war games and killed Nazis and Japs.

"I've asked him, you know, about the war but he doesn't talk about it. I asked Uncle Charlie, and Uncle Arthur, and Seamus and Danny. They all tell the same things. They talk about the chow, the weather and how their feet hurt, but they don't talk about *it*. I don't get it.

"Yes, you do, you get it plenty. He was there alright, your father. Charlie too, all of them in one way or another, but he was in the middle of it, much more so than Danny or Andrew and Seamus. He came home far more changed than the rest did. For him it was the hardest. And I can see it is for you."

My glass was almost empty, and there were no other distractions. Thomas had me right where he wanted me.

"Ahh. I'll get over it, I'm just trying to get used to, you know, workin' and like, you know, payin' bills. Stuff like that."

Thomas turned toward the mirror again and took a sip out of his beer. This time he spoke to the mirror.

"You've walked into the darkness. I can see it in your eyes son. That's the other side—and the darkness leaves its mark. The ones that have walked there—and lived—they can never see this side the same way again. They never completely get used to it as you say."

"I want to forget about that part, Seanathair, I need to."

Thomas took a moment to re-light his pipe that had gone dead in his hand. He puffed out a good cloud of smoke and pointed the stem at my image in the mirror.

"You can't and you won't. It's a hard thing—the darkness. What you saw there—was that it isn't something terrible out in front of you, but inside of you, a frightful loathsome thing, squatting deep inside of you—waiting. Seeing it and what it is capable of, it makes you afraid, and ashamed."

Shocked, I stared at the old man in the mirror his eyes meeting mine. How could he know this—about the beast? "Some things are beyond redemption Grandpa, there are things that you can't take back."

"No, you cannot take it back Mo Mhac, but the darkness is a living thing. It feeds on sorrow and regret it does. It has hunger that will eat you from the inside, and if you allow it, you will become it. A little at a time you will become—that *thing*" He paused and threw down his whiskey. "You will become—darkness itself."

I snatched my beer glass and threw back the last swallow, putting down the glass down it hit the bar harder than I had meant to, and Willy was there in a flash to refill it. This time he stayed.

"He and I don't talk. I'm pretty sure we're past that. I don't think I could, and I'm pretty sure he won't."

"Your Da holds his own counsel, but there are two sides of every coin. I see the other side from the one that you see, and you'll see it now too. A quiet man holds many secrets."

"Grandpa, you don't know how hard it is to get up close to him."

"Do you know what Mick, your father, did in the war? Do you know what his job was? Don't you think he prays for redemption? You need to talk to them, but this time you'll be speaking from where they have stood all these many years."

Willy nodded, and stayed put. Then he reached back up to the top shelf and brought down the Jamison and poured three more. Setting down the bottle on the bar, he looked down at the three glasses and spoke, almost reluctantly, "I did a full tour in Korea, you know, 1952, 1st Marine Division," and then almost reluctantly he raised his fist, "HooRah." He threw down the shot and looked me in the eye.

Suddenly, in that moment, Willy changed right before my eyes. I saw it in his eyes, as he looked into mine, I saw the irretrievable sadness, the regret—the darkness.

Then Thomas finished, "I can imagine it though, what you did, what you saw. How much of what you went through does he know about? Have you opened up with him about it? The shit that they did show us on the television was bad enough; you don't have to stretch your imagination too far to know that it was probably worse. Now you come home with that stuff that they pinned on your chest and I know they don't give you those for peeling potatoes. So how about it, Emmett, how much have you shared? You've always had a talent for collecting scars but there are more now. Your hand, and your face. I'm thinking there are more on the inside too."

He poked his finger into my chest for emphasis.

"Purgatory is for the dead, not the living Emmett. You need to find your way back home. It's time you had a talk—with him—and with them." He paused and finished his beer. "Before it's too late."

To find out more about Michael Deeze and his books, visit www.indiesunited.net/michael-deeze

Winter

HUMOR

A Heretical Guide to Classifying Beer

Timothy R. Baldwin

If you have friends like mine, you're bound to wind up at some holiday party this year. At those parties, someone will likely encourage you to try the latest beer by a local microbrewery. Your friends will grin with enthusiasm, saying, "You've got to try this!" And you'll drink out of a community cup like it's a Christmas Eve service, only no one will feign sanitizing its rim by wiping it with a white cloth. Simultaneously, your friends will boastfully proclaim the gospel of beer, using words like aromatic, assertive, or complex. You'll take them at their word, and maybe you'll agree with your friends, or perhaps you'll know instantly they're as ignorant about beer as you are. But, only if you're honest.

Growing up, I didn't know much about beer, and I can't say that I know a lot about it now. But if I did know more, I could talk to you about how beer has been ingrained in cultures throughout the world since Noah's Ark with the earliest recorded recipes dating back to 4300 BC. I could talk to you about how the ancient Egyptians brewed beer commercially and had various social traditions associated with beer, such as an Egyptian gentleman offering a lady a sip of his beer, thus announcing their betrothal. I could also talk to you about how the early brewers used balsam, hay, dandelion, and even crab claw for flavoring. I could even go into detail about beer's various uses during the Medieval period beyond its use for nutrition and celebration. These include tithing, trading, payment, and even taxing.

Furthermore, I could go into some depth about the addition of hops to the brewing process in 1000 AD and how 200 years later, it became a substantial commercial enterprise in Eastern Europe. I could even share with you some very fun facts like how kings used beer to toast victories and how Queen Elizabeth I of England drank strong ale for breakfast. Furthermore, in the colonial period, George Washington and Thomas Jefferson each had their own private brewhouses. Then, as the discussion looms upon modern history, I could even go into some depth about how before the 1800s, most beers were simply some variation of ale. And, of course, Louis Pasteur's discovery of yeast in 1876 significantly impacted the fermentation process for beer (as well as wine), thus leading to over 2300 breweries in the U.S. in 1880 and Pabst's ability, alone, to brew 1 million barrels in a year. But, I won't go into these fun historical facts because this information is easily accessible on beerhistory.com, where, in addition to a concise timeline, one can find a list of well over twenty books and articles on this very topic.

If beer were a religion, it would probably be the oldest religion in the world with various offshoots and sects preferring barley over wheat, hoppier beers versus sweeter beers, light beers over dark beers, stouts or porters over ales and lagers, and so forth. If beer were a religion, then the prophets of this religion, who describe their beers with terms like "sessionable" and "malt-driven" or "having a balanced interplay between malt and hop bitterness" would cry heresy. Furthermore, they'd burn me at the stake for refusing to adhere to their strict standards of description, all of which you can find on the Beer Style Guide at craftbeer.com.

Now, in my earlier years as a beer novice, I would have given a person a blank stare at the mention of such phrases. Though I don't anymore, and not because I lay claim to any real expert knowledge on the matter. Instead, I've experimented with various beers, mostly at parties that are just as much about trying new and exciting beers as they are about meeting new and exciting people. As a result, I've come to conclude that beers, regardless of the family in which they fall (i.e. lager, ale, stout, porter, and so forth) are like people you might meet at a party. They can fit into the following categories: *The Eccentric, The Nice Guy/Gal, The Life of the Party*, and *The Asshole.*

Hence, the almost heretical way in which I intend to set out to describe beer. I will purposefully move away from any terminology that demands some technical expertise into this world by describing beer in terms that would be more accessible to the ordinary individual who, like myself, enjoy a good beer. Therefore, the following descriptors will be added to the categories I created: *Another Round*, *I'll Drink it if There's Nothing Else*, or *Hell no!*

To demonstrate this thesis, I chose Sierra Nevada's Beer Camp Across the World, a collection of collaborative projects containing twelve different kinds of beers. For the sake of brevity and to eliminate redundancy, I have chosen four of these twelve beers to illustrate how these categories might work for the average beer drinker.

The Eccentric. Simultaneously intriguing and off-putting, the West Coast Style DIPA gives off an aroma almost identical to peeling a grapefruit. However, upon taking your first sip, you experience bursts of sweet citrus akin to biting into a slice of tangerine. The sweetness lingers for a brief moment before it's overwhelmed by the taste of sour grapefruit, causing your eyes to squint and your lips to pucker. Upon swallowing, the aftertaste is bitter, but not unbearable. This beer is very much like the eccentric person you'd meet at a party. These people hold your attention until the conversation begins to sour, veering off into topics in which you have no interest. You wonder whether this West Coast Style DIPA, boasting of 8.3% alcohol, is something you can, or even should, actually finish. But finish it you do because it feels like such a waste, this far into the pint, to stop. Not only that, but you have no one else to pass it off to, and you feel bad about leaving it alone. To this beer, you might say, "Eh... I'll drink it again if there is nothing else around."

The Nice Guy/Gal. The Dunkle Weiss, a German-Bavarian style beer, tries very hard to be well-liked. It is neither inoffensive nor off-putting. With 5.7% alcohol, this beer smells like a fresh spring breeze across a field of grass sprinkled with patches of newly blossoming flowers. Upon your first sip, you are greeted by the familiar taste of cherry candies, like the ones the old ladies at church carry in their purse. Molasses, mild and watered down, are also noticeable within your first few sips. As you continue to drink this beer, you even notice hints of cocoa powder, like the air you breathe in through your mouth while pouring hot cocoa mix into a dry mug. Upon swallowing your first sip, you experience a mild chocolatey finish, and every sip after that is consistently the same. Like the Nice Guy or Gal at the party, everyone spends some time with this beer. Some, like myself, will ask for another round, while others are content with the experience of just one. However, at some point, you will go back to this beer because it is perfectly sweet.

The Life of the Party. If the nice guy or gal should suddenly develop charisma, this person would become the one who makes everyone laugh, yet does so in a way that offends no one at all. The Atlantic Style Vintage Ale is one such beer. Upon giving it an introductory sniff, a faint plummy aroma wafts through your nostrils, much like the mist of body spray from five feet away. Upon your first sip, you are greeted by fruit punch, and you are taken back to your childhood, sitting on the back stoop in the hot sun, sipping through a straw-stuffed into a box of juice. It's pleasant. Yet there is a mild bitterness to this fruit punch taste that enhances, rather than overwhelms the experience. It is much like the taste of tonic water added to the bowl of fruit punch to liven up the drink at a dry party. This beer, with its 8.5% alcohol per volume, is a beer that everyone at the party will likely want to drink because the taste is truly something to be experienced. The harbinger of this experience - the one who encourages everyone to have a sip - will also be elevated to the same exalted level of "Life of the Party," even if he or she didn't even bring the beer. Because of the higher alcohol content and the taste, to this beer, I would say, "Another round!"

The Asshole. The Dry Hopped Barley Wine Style Ale clothes itself with the appearance of The Eccentric. The asshole has opinions. It makes various and unfounded claims, all of which are initially intriguing, but the more you are around the asshole, the more uncomfortable you feel because the asshole has complete disregard for anyone but himself. This beer gives off the sweet, citrusy aroma of orange blossoms, and you think, "Yeah! This is gonna be great!" However, when you sip it for the first time, you are reminded of that one time when you insufficiently peeled an orange and suffered the bitter consequences of chewing the remnants of said peel. However, the sweet citrus taste initially offsets the bitterness by leaving you with the aftertaste you get when you eat a sour grapefruit. Oddly, there is a mild toffee, almost caramel flavor within each sip.

Still, it's more like someone decided to further compound the taste by stuffing a Werther's Original (the chewing kind) inside a slice of the sourest grapefruit they could find. Then, after all of this, you realize how much this beer mimics The Asshole Personality. It boasts a whopping 9.4% alcohol per volume that is guaranteed to turn any well-intentioned person into an asshole should said person decides to have another round. I, for one, never want to put anything even remotely resembling this to my lips and therefore say, "Hell no!"

So from one novice to another, the preceding is a simple way of categorizing your beer. You don't have to be an acolyte, a beer connoisseur, or even a master-beer craftsman to discuss with fluency why you prefer one beer over another. Take a sip, take mental notes of its effect on your senses, and categorize the experience accordingly. But I'd recommend trying this experiment at home first with a beer sampler pack and a notebook. You do, after all, want to avoid the distraction of a pesky holiday party filled with assholes who would be delighted to lord over you their claims that they know the exact taste of a well-balanced beverage of malt and hops. Because, you know, everyone can go to the produce section of their grocery store and buy hops (whatever that is), so that they can sprinkle it on their salad, toss it into their smoothie, or eat it raw. But malt, in all seriousness, can easily be picked up. Go down the Ethnic aisle of your grocery store and pick up a few bottles labeled "malt beverage," and you will know the precise taste of malt. But, as for everything else, stick to food associations that are familiar to you. Even if some eccentric looks at you like you have a head filled with barley, the nice guy or gal and the life of the party will smile with appreciation that you even dared to describe the taste of beer in simple, everyday language.

To find out more about Timothy R. Baldwin and his books, visit
www.indiesunited.net/timothy-baldwin

LITERARY FICTION

Baby's First Book

Michael Deeze

I am restless, tired of sitting in the old wing chair without anything else to occupy my energy. I fidget, trying to find an excuse to keep sitting while not wanting to sit any longer at the same time. In frustration I rise to my feet and pace a circuit around the room, away from the heat of the fire and back again. My damaged knees protest the first steps as they always do, but gradually give up the complaint until the next time.

Encouraged, I shuffle another circuit, idly brushing my hand along crowded book shelves, full to bursting with tomes of knowledge, and children's old story books side by side. Any empty spaces that might have been, filled with keepsakes, mementos and outright junk collected over a lifetime of endeavor. All of them reminders, each one harkening back to the memory that fostered its place on a shelf of distinction.

Memories, especially old memories, have a way of

fading the color of the picture. Bright hues of summer become the pastel of memory. The happy times, bring equal parts of happiness of times gone by and sadness that they are no more. The hard times and the sad times have their sharp edges smoothed, so the contrast of sorrow becomes more grey than black. Even at a distance the pain of the hard times is unmitigated even at the great distance of time gone by and the greying of memory.

Each piece on these shelves represents a learning experience. A small piece of knowledge that, at the time, did not instantly transfer to wisdom. It was only over time that the knowledge could ferment, combining with emotions and become wisdom, often too late to serve anything but a rue-worthy moment of reflection.

Near the far end of the shelves, in the darkest corner of the room; one book draws my eyes with each shuffling revolution of the room. I know it by heart, its feel and the undeniable weight of it. Pausing, I glide my index finger down the spine, slowly mouthing the title; Baby's First Book.

Sliding the leatherette album out I carry it to the chair. With it resting on my lap, I look at the filigreed beadwork cover, running my fingers over its texture.

I woke the boys before daylight.

"C'mon guys! Mom says it's time."

In an instant they were both out of bed and pulling on clothes. We had been ready for this, the last two weeks; a seeming eternity. At last, it was time and my excitement equaled theirs.

Once downstairs, their shoes and jackets were pulled on near the back door. Only then did my wife appear, coming down the stairs. The look on her face did not match the excited anticipation of the three of us. She grimaced as her foot struck the floor, and her eyes were wide with something else.

"Something's wrong, Em."

"Wrong how?"

"I don't know, just not right. We need to go."

The boys were dancing at the door, eager to go. I lifted the small travel bag that we'd packed days ago and I helped Greta out the door and down the back-porch steps. Once situated in the truck we started the thirty-minute drive to town so we could meet our newest family member.

I understood her trepidation. There had been other babies. Other little ones that had not made it to the finish line. Each one, loved from the moment of conception, but ultimately not ready for this world. Each one grieved for once they were no more. For their mother, it was a bottomless feeling of loss and failure that relentlessly ebbed and flowed like the tides with the changing of the moon. For me the father, it was a struggle to locate the grief and deal with it on a conscious level—Struggling with the inability to console my wife, because nothing can fill the hole that such a loss creates. There had been other little souls.

My hands tightened on the steering wheel, mitigating the concern with the excitement of the potential moment. Encouraging the boys with their suggestions for names of the new arrival.

"Skuzz-bucket." Seth was wide awake and looking for a laugh.

"How 'bout Cheez-Wiz?" I said. "With a name like that, he'd be sure to be a major NBA Superstar."

"How 'bout you shuddup? It's gonna be a girl." Grit was playing along between contractions.

"I know, I'm all set. Wilhelmina is my vote."

"You are such a dipshit. We already decided, it's gonna be Jennie. Jennifer Lee."

"*You* decided, you mean."

"Same difference."

I had called ahead to the hospital. I had been working in and around the hospital for the last ten years so I wasn't surprised when no one but my very good friend Paulette Downing met us as we entered through the ER doors.

"I'm so excited for you Doc! Grit how'ya doin', baby? Your folks are gonna be so excited. Come on, honey, I'll take you back. Doc, take the kids into the chapel. I already laid out some snacks and pillows so they can sack out once they're done."

"Thanks, Paulie. Any word on Doc Southerland?"

"He's passed the puck, Doc. You got none other than Doctor Kearney tonight," he insisted.

Paulette and Greta headed through the double doors and into the hospital proper just as Jim Kearney was getting ready to step through.

"Hey Emmett! How about this? Another delivery, only this time it's yours. I'm thankful that I can be a part of it, especially after the others." He narrowed his brows and put a hand on my shoulder.

"Grit says there's something wrong."

"What? What do you mean?" He was immediately on the alert.

"She said she doesn't know. Just …not right."

"Okay, I'm heading back right away. Go scrub up, Emmett. I'll catch you up once you're down there."

There was no way to hurry up scrubbing up and getting into scrubs but I shaved the corners a little anyway. Even so, as I turned down the hall leading to the one maternity delivery room, I met Paulette and Jim coming the other way.

"Get Randy on the phone right away, and also Doctor Epstein, we need anesthesia too. Call in the surgical team and prep the room, Paulette." Turning to me, he continued, "Sorry Emmett, I can't let you go down right now. We've got some issues and we need to move quickly. Baby's in distress, and Grit's B.P. is off the charts. Two hundred ten over one-seventy. We need to take your baby right away."

"Eclampsia." I didn't have to guess. I had seen first-hand what kind of hell it could cause.

"Exactly. We need to go; I'm going to scrub up. I hope they find Randy in town; I don't know what his surgical schedule is these days."

"I'll check on the boys, then. Are you sure I can't help calm her down, Jim?"

"She's afraid you'll be more upset than she is. The last time was bad enough, Emmett; she's afraid, and this time she's right."

"That's nuts. Sorry Jim, I'm going to go see her."

"Okay, we'll get ready."

Holding her hand while she tried to control her breathing, I met her gaze.

"This is like before, Emmett. Oh God, we're so close. I can't do that again."

She was mirroring my own feelings. We had suffered miscarriages in the past, more than a few. Each one had been hard, but none had gotten beyond twelve to fifteen weeks. With this pregnancy, everything had gone right. Grit had gotten more beautiful with each passing week, and we had laughed and enjoyed the planning and preparations. Now we were at forty weeks, full term, the finish line.

"It's okay my love, it's just a speed bump. I won't let anything happen to you or to the baby. It's gonna be all right. We've got Paulette and Jim right here, and I wouldn't be surprised if that dipshit Tom Dunbar doesn't blow through the doors any minute now too. We're in good hands."

"I know, but I'm still scared. I feel terrible."

Paulette entered briskly and once the door was open wide, a surgical gurney followed her into the room, pushed by one of the surgical team.

"Doc, sorry but you've got to scrub again. We can't find Epstein. Randy's already here, so we're gonna need the extra hand."

"No Paulette, I can't. I just can't do that. C'mon, what about Tom?"

"I tried that. I talked to Janet. She says he's had to take his pain meds twice tonight and he's finally resting. We can't use him."

A shuddering gasp came from behind us. This from Grit.

Everyone in the room was galvanized by the spectacle taking place on the bed. My wife was in full rigorous spasm, her shoulders and heels the only thing making contact with the bed itself. Her pelvis and swollen abdomen thrust toward the ceiling. Her eyes rolled back in her head.

"Code Blue!" Paulette yelled and pushed a button above the headboard.

A calm female voice spoke over the hospital intercom, "Code Blue, maternity. Code Blue, maternity, Code Blue, maternity."

"Let's go!" This was not her first rodeo; Paulette was in command. "Doc, other side- pull the sheet. On the count of three, lift: one, two, three." We lifted, and heaved her onto the gurney. Almost before she had settled, the sides came up and the surgical nurse headed for the door.

"Doc, go ahead of us. We'll see you in there. Epstein's gonna have some serious hell to pay once I find him."

Hours later I quietly entered the little hospital chapel. Pausing at the altar in front of me, I looked up at the benevolent gaze of the Man on the Cross for a long moment as he looked back at me. Turning to the two small boys asleep on the pews in front of him I sat down between them, and touched Seth on the shoulder. He opened his eyes, rolling them in sleepy awareness.

"Is she here?"

"Yeah, Dad, is it really a girl?" This from his brother Sean.

"It is a girl, boys." I idly stroked Sean's hair as I smiled down at him.

"Can we go see her now?" There was excitement but sleepy excitement.

"I'm afraid she couldn't make it all the way out of heaven, boys. I'm sorry."

Sitting back down in the chair near the fire I open the little book. Turning from one empty page to the next, all of them blank. A study in cream colored heavy bond paper. The little Baby's First Book has no entries, no recounted life events, no landmark dates. The pages, like her experiences, still blank after all these years.

To find out more about Michael Deeze and his books, visit
www.indiesunited.net/michael-deeze

PARANORMAL HORROR

Dark Holiday

JB Murray

He knew the roads were icy before they'd even left the lodge. The weatherman said a storm was rising, blowing in from Canada, crashing into another front coming from the west, and was sure to blanket the northeast in a centuries' new record snowfall.

The day had been warm though; pleasant. But as the clouds rolled in, they brought with them the slightest rain.

Then the temperatures dropped.

The snow started.

But all in all, it had been a great holiday getaway from the life he and Samantha were accustomed to. They'd spent so much time worrying, they'd almost lost themselves. Worrying about the bills, and what came next. Diving headlong into long days of work, taking up extra hours just to get by; each working as hard as they could on their careers they spent less and less time together. Jarrod came home one evening, following a day much like this and realized, he almost didn't recognize her anymore. When had she changed her hair color? When had she cut it? And when was it that she forgot how to smile?

It broke his heart, that moment of realization. But it woke something as well. And he'd decided then and there, they needed to get away. They needed time. Time to breathe. Time to live. Time to remember why they'd fallen for each other in the first place.

It was light, the snow. A soft fluffy blanket at first; the flakes being whisked away from the tires of Jarrod's SUV. Both hands on the wheel. The traction control on his vehicle managed the occasional slippage here and there as they snaked through the endless roads in this back country, a canopy of trees lining either side of them. His wife sat quietly in the passenger's seat, a book opened on her lap, glasses hanging just on the tip of her nose like she often did when she read, as if she wasn't really looking through them at all, but rather over them. It was an endearing trait that he always found amusing. The set of her glasses. The way she twirled her hair around one finger and sometimes chewed it when she was really enthralled with a book; the way she bit her lower lip when she was nervous; the way her eyes always darted to the floor, then looked up at him without moving her head, a smile playing across her mouth when she was horny. Somehow, it was the simple things like that, that always felt like home, even if their home had become a forgotten thing. They'd dated only a year, marrying the year after, and were now on their third. But he remembered thinking, even back then, that within seconds of those first smiling moments, everything about her seemed to fit. And nothing felt quite like home to him, as his Samantha.

A slight smile appeared on her face, her cheeks crawling upward as she turned her head and glanced at him over her glasses. Like always, she had known he'd been watching her. He smiled back. Winked. Samantha giggled that one of a kind giggle where she shook her head slightly from side to side and covered her mouth with her fingers. It was an almost child-like gesture, purely innocent. She mouthed the words "I love you" through that smile of hers. Taking one hand from the wheel, he reached over and grabbed one of hers. He pulled it to him, kissing the top of her hand, and held it to his cheek. Closed his eyes for just a moment, breathing in the smell of her skin.

His hand on the steering wheel slipped violently to the left as the wheels suddenly caught a long patch of ice. Everything that happened next slowed down more than just a fraction.

Like living a lifetime in a matter of seconds.

He let go of her hand and reached for the wheel, his unconscious mind preparing to take over and steer them to safety.

Jarrod glanced over as Samantha's glasses fell from her face and she reached out for the dashboard with one hand, gripping the passenger's side door with the other. Her smile had contorted into a mask of fear; eyes bulging wide, mouth perched to scream.

The SUV skid sideways for a moment, and next he knew they were backwards, and he was looking out the windshield at the road they had just traversed. The force of the skid kept him pinned against the armrest.

A carousel ensued, as the vehicle spun.

A tree lined forest.

Banks of white.

The road.

More trees.

The road again.

That sickening feeling of lost control. His chest crushed under the immense weight of centrifugal force. And as the vehicle swung around once more, he caught only a glimpse of it. But the glimpse was all he needed.

The outcropping of boulders by the roadside, just barely peeking out from under the snow. Boulders, just a bit taller than the tires on his SUV. *How fast were they spinning?30?40?50? Faster?* He had been going at least 40 before the wheels slid out from under him just moments before.

Sideways again. He craned his neck, working against the force of the spin, the cords standing out, as he attempted to look at Samantha. She, herself was pinned to the passenger's side door.

Jarrod closed his eyes.

Knew it was coming.

And then suddenly it was as if someone had turned off the volume to the world. The screams, the whooshing of the wind, the SUV engine, all fell silent for just a second.

CRACK!

Bent metal.

No longer pinned to their seats, but upward now, the seatbelt digging into their shoulders. They were falling upside down, for the briefest of moments. The belts anchoring them painfully.

Jarrod watched the world turn upside down as the SUV struck the boulders and flipped. The forest whirled by, a kaleidoscope of pine greens, bare brown branches, and flutters of snow.

Turning.

Rotating.

No sound, but the last gasp of his wife and the tires spinning furiously in mid-air. As the SUV flipped into the woods, he knew they were now at the mercy of fate, and fate alone.

The SUV landed first on its roof, in a clearing just large enough to fit the vehicle, before bouncing down a slight grade. The roof concaved. Windows exploding, the hood bounced open like a trapdoor and ripped off as the front axle snapped and a tire went rolling ahead. The truck turned over and over and Jarrod could swear, that one momentary glimpse out the side window, looking to his left, that he could see the immense pine coming toward them at breakneck speed. Then the SUV smashed into the tree, just beyond the front tire of the passenger's side.

There was a crunch.

A thud.

The SUV struck the tree, lurching up to one side, and then fell back into place, stopping abruptly.

It took a moment for the haze to lift. Jarrod shook his head and looked up, the cobwebs falling from his vision, though not quickly enough.

A ringing in his ears.

He was freezing.

His window had been smashed, and snow was blowing in through it. Frantically he looked to his right. He could feel one eye swelling shut, and from the other he had to wipe a warm trickle of fluid that had cascaded into his eye, staining his vision in crimson. But Samantha was not there in the passenger's seat.

He coughed; swallowed back something coppery and sweet. Reached for the door handle and tugged at it. Amazingly enough, the door was free and swung open. Jarrod fumbled a moment with the clasp on his seatbelt. Moments later he clicked free. Thank goodness for small miracles. He didn't as much as step out of the truck as fell out, landing on his hands and knees. The snow was considerably deeper now. Nearly up to his shoulders in this canine position.

Jarrod wrenched his head up, his neck stiff from impact. Even in the dense wood, he could see it was coming down much faster now. The snow. Stumbling, he got to his feet, and using the truck as a crutch, he walked around to the passenger's side and pried open the door.

Senses coming back to him now.

Adrenalin rushed through him, warming him slightly and helping to clarify his thoughts. The passenger's seat *was* empty. He hadn't imagined it.

Stepped away from the vehicle a matter of feet, and looked around him, surveying the wreckage. The scene of the accident.

There in the snow, just past the tree with which the SUV had collided, sat her book. The one she'd been reading. It teetered on its edge, partly covered in white as if it threatened to fall deeper at a moment's notice. He stammered forward and picked it from the ground. There were specs of crimson on the cover. Brushed one hand against the fabric of it, turning it this way and that, his eyes trying to focus. And that's when he saw it; a trail.

Droplets of cherry red wine were spattered here and there on the snowy white linen of the forest floor, leading from where the book had sat aloft the powder, deeper into the woods. *Had she gotten out by herself and walked off in that direction?* But there were no footprints.

He slipped the paperback into his back pocket, and without thinking much now of his own safety, the matter of finding Samantha winning over, trudged out into the woods to find her.

Couldn't tell how long he'd been walking. The silence in the wood made everything deafening. Each time the wind picked up he could feel it to his core. Slicing at his skin; gnawing at the bone. Clumps of snow falling from the branches almost seemed to echo in the infinity of the forest.

He walked at first.

Then, his pace quickened, and his heart raced. Little by little, he sped faster and faster into the unknown. A desperate man on an even more desperate mission. A man with no compass but that within his heart. That which called out for his wife. His love. His Samantha.

Without warning, the trail ceased. He looked left, then right; ahead and behind. The ground was untouched. He spun on the heel. His head reeled. His eyes barely focused as the trees twirled by in a blur. *Where was the trail? Where had the breadcrumbs gone?*

The trees around began to spin a little faster as a brief bout of panic set in. He turned this way and that. *Where the hell was she?* Jarrod screamed.

He fell to his knees and began to cry. His tears nearly froze to his face. The hope which had pushed him this far turned cold and bitter as well, lost somewhere in the icy breeze. He stayed there a bit, on his knees, trying not to cry, trying not to think of the pain that was currently rushing through his scalp. He rubbed away the blood again from his eye. He could feel a swatch of skin roll and fold against his touch, surprised it wasn't flapping in the wind. Sighed.

Moments later, he felt the oddest of things. It was the warmest of breezes. Almost like a breath against his skin. In it, he could smell embers, cinnamon, and pine. Warm, like home. He looked up, confused. The breeze had halted. But ahead in the woods stood… a man? *Was it a man?* Tall, dark hair, with eyes of a crystal blue he'd swear. Though he couldn't quite make out his clothes. They seemed almost to be made of the snow that fell around him. Jarrod rubbed his eyes, once. Twice. The man was still there.

He smiled at Jarrod.

Was he pointing? Yes, yes he was! He was directing Jarrod. Hastily Jarrod jumped to his feet, stumbling over a bit, nearly crashing back down into the powder around him. When he righted himself, the man was gone. *Had he imagined him?* No, certainly not. His feet were moving before he could command them to. He trotted in the direction in which the man had pointed.

Running now.

Jarrod ran hard and fast as the woods around grew denser and denser still, it almost seemed to close in around him.

Bounced off one tree with his shoulder.

They were surrounding him.

He stopped and started. Taking a few weary steps. Stopped again. They were closing in. The dark husk of their bark seemed to absorb all light. Started again, walking sideways, then forward. A man on confused and nervous legs.

He was walking, as briskly as he could, skirting this way and that through the trees, each only a matter of a foot apart now, their trunks stretching into the heavens, their branches so high above reaching out in all directions, strangling all the light of day.

Jarrod looked back and could not see behind him.

Caught in this labyrinth.

But still, he moved forward, something pulling him, almost beckoning. And then, just as sudden as the memory of the SUV slamming against the boulder, he came to a clearing.

The space was huge, vacant, and he could see the trees circling around, creating a cul-de-sac of sorts. And there, in the middle, lay something. He need not see it up close, as he knew what it was. He knew the light brown jacket and the feathery hood even from here. He knew the long black hair fanning out against the snow.

Jarrod took off at an unbelievable pace. Snow kicked up behind him off his boots.

His Samantha!

Yes!

He knew without knowing. He could taste her in the air, sense all that was her, and like a magnet, was drawn to her. And then he was upon her. Skidding to a halt. Looked away. His breath caught in his throat, a sickening feeling clutching at his gut. His eyes filled with tears. Looked back slowly, and there she lay, sprawled out on the snow like a rag doll.

Her body bent and twisted.

Face contorted; frozen in a disgusting, vile grimace.

As he knelt near her, Jarrod began to sob and scooped her up in his arms. The warmth had left her completely now, and she was stiff, heavy. He screamed again. Lowered his face to hers and cried an eternity's worth of tears.

A warm breeze flittered by. Cinnamon. Pine. Embers.

Jarrod looked up from his wife's corpse. The man was standing over him. Only he looked older this close. He was tall, yes. *His hair dark?* Yes. But his face was sunken, shallow, almost cutting. His eyes were vacant and hollow. He glowed faintly there in the snow. And the flakes seemed almost to rest upon his shoulders, then cascade down and off his back, a shimmering cape of white crystals. The stranger smiled down at Jarrod. Jarrod returned in kind. *Was this a hallucination? Who was this stranger? A figment of imagination? An apparition? Maybe… an angel?*

"Are you," Jarrod stuttered against the cold, breathing in the warmth that seemed to surround this man that stood before him. "Are you… an angel?"

The stranger retorted, though his lips never parted, and his mouth hadn't moved. The words flowed not from him exactly as they seemed to come from the howling wind. But the smile never left the stranger's face.

"Not exactly," the stranger whispered.

To find out more about JB Murray and his books, visit
www.indiesunited.net/jb-murray

NARRATIVE FICTION

Gumbo

Aaron S Gallagher

"Mother, I've brought the papers. We can go over them and get them signed," Caleb said.

The kitchen's windows were frosted white from steam. Hot water seared strong, calloused hands as they scrubbed vegetables, lining the heavy maple block. She crushed a bulb of garlic over the sink, rolling it between loose hands. She separated the cloves, chose five. She clasped hands to her face, inhaling the fresh biting scent. Her seamed and wrinkled hands resembled the board, whose surface scars told the history of her kitchen. Every meal, every day, every year writ there, if you knew how to read them. Exactly like her hands. The cutting board, built with his own hands, then strong and fine, neither seamed nor cracked.

She stropped her heavy knife, five strokes on one side, four on the other. Three on the one side, two on the other, one on the one side, and tap the steel with the backbone of the blade for good luck the way her mother had.

"Mother, please pay attention," Caleb said. "This is important."

The carbon steel seemed sharp enough to carve the air. She dissected the onion, her practiced hands making short work of its concentric rings and stinging depths. A double-handful of diced onions went into the first bowl. The peppers came next. Into the second bowl went the peppers, each piece identical, a mounded pile of rectangular chunks. She sliced the okra into medallions and set it on a paper towel to absorb some of the slime.

The celery sliced with a pleasurable ease. Celery begged to be sliced, the vacant, upturned smiles beaming at her from the board. Into the smallest bowl she piled the celery. It always amused her, how one onion became more than two peppers, than three stalks of celery. The bowls shrank as the numbers of increased.

Her mother's good, heavy cast iron Dutch oven with its glassy, rock-polish cure went onto the stove. No soap had touched that surface in a hundred years. Nothing survived on that inexorable surface. Nothing adhered. She wished she were as cured as the iron. She turned the gas on high, waiting until she smelled the rotten-egg stink before popping the sulfur match alight with her thumbnail. A mushroom cloud of flame enveloped the pot, adding carbon to the rough pebbled exterior. She turned the flame low, then up a touch.

"Every time," Caleb said. "You do it that way every time."

She nodded.

"Why?"

It had always delighted her. The infantile pleasure she took in the flump and pop of gas ignition. A childish delight. Some things still brought pleasure.

She poured oil into the Dutch oven and waited for it to begin to move before she emptied the paper towel. Okra sizzled and jumped. She let it fry for a couple of minutes, stirring with a wooden spoon at least as old as Caleb, the grain standing out like the veins on the backs of her ancient hands. Once the okra was sufficiently prepped she scooped it from the pot back onto the paper towel. She added more oil to the cast iron, measuring by eye, and then flour. She stirred her own cauldron.

Caleb said, "You don't need to do this. There's more important things to worry about."

She took care that every speck of flour blended into the oil.

"We have paperwork to look at. Things to sign. Things more important to do," Caleb said again. "We don't need it. There's going to be plenty of food tomorrow."

She bent to peer at the flame, turned it up just a hair. Not enough that Caleb could tell anything had changed, but it had. She knew. She knew. It had changed.

"Fine, then. That's going to take hours," Caleb tried again. "We can get some of the details taken care of. We have to-"

She watched the roux, imagining the flour heating, darkening. The rich, nutty flavor stretching into the oil like threads. The roux thickened, darkened. She stirred, following the pattern with absent, practiced ease. Around the outside counter-clockwise three times and then in a figure-eight, an infinity sign, until she had scraped each grain of the silky roux from the embrace of the cured iron.

"I know why you're doing this," he said. "Acting like this."

Was it chocolate now? So close. She licked her lips. It was almost… there. Milk chocolate. A color she could never quite explain but knew when she saw it. Almost time now.

"Mother, you need to pay attention."

She did need to pay attention or the roux would turn on her. You had but a second with perfection before you lost it. A moment, and before you knew it all was lost. That's all it took. You looked away and you lost it. Whether it was a second or thirty-three years.

And… <u>now</u>. That perfect balance between milk chocolate and dark chocolate. Still smooth before that moment when it turned: burned; became granular and useless. She reached without looking, poured the celery into the roux, reveling in the angry hiss. She tapped the bowl against the side of the iron pot. She set the bowl back in its place next to the cutting board. The board and butcher's block had been made from the same trees, scrap pieces of the wood that held up this very house. He'd built it himself, built all of it with his bare hands.

Celery sizzled as she stirred and stirred, her hand snaking out almost without her noticing, to gather a healthy pinch of salt.

"Could you stop that please?" Caleb asked. "I'm talking about important things."

She stirred in silence as the celery softened. The salt brought out the moisture of the celery and that pungent scent once again filled the kitchen, as it had God alone knew how many times, how many years. As the celery browned, in went the peppers and the onions, each bowl tapped against the side of the cast iron three times as defense against stubborn resistance. As the celery, peppers, onions, salt, and roux mixed in that alchemical reaction, she fancied she could see the moment when food and love combined to make a meal. She stirred, stirred, stirred.

"Mom," Caleb prompted. He rattled a sheaf of papers and waited. She didn't react.

After the onions she added broth to the pot, dowsing the mixture and sending up a hiss and a cloud of steam. She turned the flame to a minimal flicker of blue-white and went to the cutting board again. A platter of meat awaited her attentions. She sliced the boudin, the milky-white skins of the casing split and separated. She gathered the split casings up and added them to the compost pile near the sink. The boudin disbursed into the broth to thicken and flavor.

"Mom, we need to take care of this," Caleb said. "It's time-sensitive."

She worked with neat efficiency. The flavor was time-sensitive. The gumbo tasted best when it heated the meat, rather than adding meat to a hot pot of broth. It mattered, the order in which things were done. Andouille next, after she sliced the sacred sausage into medallions, the white of gristle and fat tiny flecks in the red of the meat. The andouille would plump as it cooked, the red-brown flesh growing tight and the skin hardening like salami. She popped a piece into her mouth, savoring the slow heat and bite of the spices. She steeled herself to working with the chicken breasts. They were her least favorite, even over tripe. The slick-smooth meat set her teeth on edge. She abhorred the rubbery, watery flesh of chicken. But she had to, ignoring the slippery-slick feel, the bright yellow-white fat. Alvin had always cut them for her.

"Mom, come on," Caleb interrupted. "Pay attention."

She dashed the errant thought away and cubed the chicken. How many chickens had been dissected on this board over thirty-three years? She pushed the chicken onto the blade of her knife and into the bubbling broth. She stirred, enjoying the savory smell. She ran her hands under water, wiped them on the blue-and-white towel tucked into her apron at her waist, and rummaged in the cabinet. She found her bay leaves and dropped three into the broth, and pushed them under the surface.

"Mom, come on. Be reasonable. This has to get done. *You* have to do it. There isn't anyone else," Caleb said.

She stirred, scraping the bottom. She closed her eyes and inhaled the sharp tang of the broth. Her kitchen smelled like heaven. Her kitchen. Hers. Hers *alone.*

She opened her eyes, blinking to stave off more tears. She topped the pot with more broth, bringing the level almost to the lip. She stirred once more and covered it. When the meal was done and the leftovers were away in the refrigerator to season, Alvin had always fetched the heavy iron to its place on the top shelf. She couldn't lift it by herself.

She stared out the window, filmy with condensation.

"You can't pretend nothing is wrong, Mama," Caleb said. "You need to deal with this."

How would she deal with this burden? She couldn't lift it on her own. She *never* had carried it on her own. Caleb had fetched the pot down from its home, but come later, come tomorrow, he'd be gone again. She stared at the trees, the fence in the distance. The leaves were dying in the chill of late fall. She and Alvin had loved fall. The crunch of the leaves and the cinnamon smell. The sign that a season had ended. Fall was a doorway through which one stepped to find winter. And when winter's door opened, you'd find spring there waiting. They had walked through hundreds of doors together. This door was hers. No one would open it for her, as a gentleman should. No one would accompany her through, one hand at the base of her back, the other gesturing before her. No one would ever lift her over the threshold the way Alvin had in a house he'd lived in every day of his marriage with her. She would live here now without him.

The meals this Dutch oven had made for them.

Of all of the dishes she had brought to life in its black, seasoned depths, gumbo had been Alvin's favorite. He would have eaten it every day of his life.

She would have to find a new place. The old place fit no longer; she could not reach it. Perhaps she would put it under the cabinet or in the pantry. A different place, a new home.

To find out more about Aaron S Gallagher and his books, visit
www.indiesunited.net/aaron-gallagher

NONFICTION

Today

Lisa Orban

In December of 2015, shortly before Christmas, my father was taken off life support. In the early morning, unable to sleep, I penned this as my final farewell to my Dad. The holidays can be a hard time for people, to lose someone so close to Christmas makes it even harder. For all of you out there who have lost someone and are struggling to put into words the grief that you feel, maybe mine can help.

My Father will die today.

In a few hours, as the sun comes up, I will get out of bed. Like every other morning I will start the coffee, and take a shower, brush my teeth and my hair. I will pick out clothes to wear. I will pick out something that I won't mind ever not wearing again, for today is the day my father will die.

Today, I will get into my car and drive to the hospital, like I have done every day for a month. I will go into my Father's room and tell him again that I love him. I will hold his hand and tell him it's going to be okay. It's important to say these things because I will never again have the chance to tell him. Because today is the day my Father is going to die.

Today, the hospital staff will come in, and with quiet words, tell us that they are going to turn off the machines that have kept him alive this last month. They will pat our shoulders and say words that they hope will help. Because they too know that today is the day my father will die and they want to help, but know that they cannot no matter how much they try.

Today, I want my Father to know that I forgave him for my childhood, many years ago. I never told him out loud before, I guess I didn't think I needed to. But I have. I think it's important now for him to know, to have no doubts when he leaves us, to know that. I want him to know how much I have grown to like him as a person, that I understand now that when I was growing up he suffered from severe anxiety and it was fear that made him act the way he did. I want him to know that I am thankful he had the courage to get the help he needed that allowed us to have a relationship as adults that had not been possible when I was a child. It's important that he knows this, because today is the day my Father is going to die, and I do not want to be one of his regrets.

Today, I will tell my Father all the things I never said out loud, because I always thought I would have time. I will remind him of the times he made me laugh, and the last lunch we had together, the times he stood up for me and the times he made me proud. Because today is the day my Father is going to die, and I will never have the chance to do so again.

Today I will smile and celebrate my Father's life. I will stand strong for my family, and I will say the words that will help them deal with their grief. For today their father, husband, brother, uncle and grandfather will die.

And tomorrow, I will cry, for my Father died today, and I will never see him again. I will never again be able to pick up the phone and talk to him. I will never again sit terrified in the passenger seat while my Father sits behind the wheel of his truck. I will never again take him to lunch or be able to invite him over to my home, for anything. He will never again sneak a brat or a beer behind my stepmother's back while begging me not to tattle on him. I will never again look up to my strong Father and see him smile back at me.

My Father will die today and I will miss him.

To find out more about Lisa Orban and her books, visit www.indiesunited.net/lisa-orban

Thank you for taking the time to read this collection from the authors of Indies United Publishing House. We hope you enjoyed it and would like to encourage you to take a moment to review this collection on your favorite reading platform.

A little about Indies United

Here at Indies United, we are a co-op of like-minded authors working together to showcase our books and highlight our diversity as writers. We openly encourage and support both new and established authors in their pursuit of finding their audience while bringing to you books worth reading. Our goal is to give authors a home to call their own, while bringing fresh, innovative, and exciting books to readers all over the world.

If you are an author, please check us out at www.indiesunited.net

If you would like to connect to Indies United you can find us at:

Facebook
https://www.facebook.com/IndiesUnitedPublishing
OR @IndiesUnitedPublishing

Twitter
https://twitter.com/IndiesUnitedPub
OR @IndiesUnitedPub

Instagram
https://www.instagram.com/lisaorbanauthor/

Linkedin
www.linkedin.com/in/indies-united-publishing-house

Pinterest
https://www.pinterest.com/indiesunited/

GoodReads
https://www.goodreads.com/user/show/122472367-indies-united